Twayne's English Authors Series

EDITOR OF THIS VOLUME

Kinley E. Roby

Northeastern University

Roy Fuller

TEAS 253

ROY FULLER

By ALLAN E. AUSTIN
University of Guelph

TWAYNE PUBLISHERS

A DIVISION OF G. K. HALL & CO., BOSTON

Published in 1979 by Twayne Publishers,
A Division of G. K. Hall & Co.
All Rights Reserved

Printed on permanent / durable acid-free paper and bound
in the United States of America

First Printing

Frontispiece photo of Roy Fuller by B. G. Potter

Library of Congress Cataloging in Publication Data
Austin, Allan E
Roy Fuller.
(Twayne's English authors series; TEAS 253)
Bibliography: p. 140–41
Includes index.
1. Fuller, Roy Broadbent, 1912-   —Criticism
and interpretation.
PR6011.U55Z55   828'.9'1209   78-11794
ISBN 0-8057-6743-6

For Margaret
Jeff and Pree

Contents

About the Author

Allan E. Austin is an Associate Professor of English at the University of Guelph, Guelph, Ontario. A journalist and freelance writer in Canada for several years before beginning his academic career, he has taught at the University of Rochester and Russell Sage College. Twentieth century British literature is his field. He is the author of the Twayne volume, *Elizabeth Bowen,* and has written on the shorter fiction of D. H. Lawrence. He is married and has two children.

Preface

Roy Fuller has been before the British public for more than forty years as poet, novelist, essayist, critic, and, more recently, as professor of poetry at Oxford. He is the only significant figure to be associated with both the central movement of British poetry in the thirties and the corresponding one in the fifties. As such his place in the tradition is secure.

While Fuller's reputation in England has always been commendable, it has continually risen, a fact attesting to his dedication to self-development and unceasing openness to both his times and the resources of his art. His commitment to high standards, evident indirectly in his work and directly in his polemic, has made him, as numerous British critics acknowledge, a presence of incalculable value in recent decades.

My references have been to Fuller's British recognition and reputation because he is relatively unknown in North America, and then almost exclusively as a poet. Much has been written about him in England, though even there not in an extended or comprehensive way. The combination, then, of Fuller's significance in Britain and limited recognition in America justify this study in theory. I am hopeful the study justifies itself in practice.

I can relate the origins of this book by retailing an anecdote of considerable embarrassment to myself. Because I was an admirer of Fuller's poetry in a casual way, I was delighted when he came to my university to give two lectures in 1971 as part of a tour of several Ontario universities he was making under the aegis of the British Council just at the time he was nearing the end of his five-year term as professor of poetry at Oxford. He proved a man of wit and warmth, and this volume's photo attests to his dapper attractiveness. When it was decided that someone from my department should drive him to his next speaking engagement at McMaster University in nearby Hamilton I promptly volunteered, welcoming the opportunity for a private tête-à-tête. During the course of that conversation Fuller raised the topic of his fiction. Fiction?! I experienced a moment of genuine alarm and then heard myself admitting ignorance of his novels—this to an author who had published eight of them. Of course Fuller smoothly alleviated any possibility of further embarrassment on my part. Actually he gave the impression of not being greatly surprised, and his subsequent remarks disclosed some resignation to the fact that his fiction has never enjoyed the degree of response accorded his poetry.

To complete my story: after having escorted Fuller to the Department of English at McMaster I decided to browse in the campus bookstore before driving home. I had not the slightest thought of looking for a Fuller novel but on this fateful day I came upon one in a Penguin paperback and bought it. Two weeks later I received a package from England containing another Fuller novel and a note from the author thanking me for my consideration. I read these novels, the other six (by now a full-fledged Fullerian), had to know what had been said about him . . . and so, naturally, to the work in your hands. If this is a form of expiation for initial ignorance, then it is a singularly rewarding one for me.

The seven chapters grow one out of the other. The first traces the progress of Fuller's life and career and provides the appropriate contexts, historical and literary, for a meaningful orientation to the creative work. The following three chapters deal chronologically with his successive volumes of poetry and note the development and permutations. In the interest of organizational clarity the poems within individual volumes have been grouped thematically and accordingly have not been dealt with sequentially. The fifth chapter discusses the novels chronologically; the sixth examines the two volumes of Oxford lectures; and the seventh provides a brief summing up.

I would like to acknowledge some of the debts I have incurred while writing this volume. May I express my sincere thanks to the Canada Council for a grant enabling me to visit London for interviews with Roy Fuller; to Roy Fuller who gave of his time generously and with gracious cordiality; to my colleague James Harrison and to my editor Kinley E. Roby, both of whom contributed suggestions with great tact.

ALLAN E. AUSTIN

University of Guelph

Acknowledgments

I would like to thank the following for permission to quote from the work of Roy Fuller: Roy Fuller, Dufour Editions, Andre Deutsch and St. Martin's Press.

Chronology

CHAPTER 1

Context and Career

I The Double Life

R OY Broadbent Fuller was born in 1912 in Failsworth, Lancashire, into a lower-middle-class milieu, to Leopold Charles and Nellie (Broadbent) Fuller. His father, who had worked his way up with a rubber-proofing firm, died as a young man when his son was eight. When he was ten Fuller moved with his mother and a brother to Blackpool where he was educated at Blackpool High School. Fuller characterizes his early life as "provincial," his background as "non-literary," his schooling as "uninspired," and his further education as "truncated."[1] While feeling an affinity for industrial Lancashire, Fuller did not care for the seaside community of Blackpool "which had no integrated social background" and he was eager to escape, specifically to London.[2] At sixteen he was articled to a solicitor; at twenty-one he passed his final exams and became qualified. For a time he was involved with local left-wing intellectual groups—"disseminating leaflets and selling the *Daily Worker*"— but, as he remarks, "Being a lawyer and being politically active was a very difficult business. My political involvement, in the sense of being involved in day-to-day politics, occupied a comparatively short period. . . . My sympathy with the working class movements was largely theoretical after about 1935, but I never lost . . . the fundamental belief in socialism and the materialistic conception of history."[3]

Fuller's early poetic education was modest, "for at that time the verse anthologies included in the set books for matriculation took one no further than Margaret L. Woods and John Drinkwater."[4] But Fuller, a voracious reader in any case, surmounted this formal cultural lag with private reading, and by 1928 he was familiar with the work of Pound and Eliot. This verse proved highly congenial to him, for it "seemed to echo and embody . . . adolescent protext to the conformities of middle-class life."[5] In this same year he had his first taste of publication, placing a poem in the Poet's Corner of the *Sunday Referee*, a launching pad also enjoyed by Dylan Thomas and Pamela Hansford Johnson. Soon he was well immersed in the thirties poetic ferment, excited by the political commitment of W. H. Auden and Stephen Spender. He continued to circulate poems, secured publication in several small magazines, and eventually attracted the attention of Geoffrey Grigson, editor of *New Verse,* John Lehmann, editor of *Penguin New Writing*, and Julian Symons, editor of *Twentieth Century Verse*, all of whom both published his work and encouraged him. These contacts also provided his first opportunities as a reviewer.

Fuller had the desired opportunity to move south, if not to London, in 1935 when he joined a firm of solicitors in Ashford, Kent. A year later he married Kathleen Smith. Then, virtually on the eve of the outbreak of World War II, and shortly after the birth of a son John, they moved to London when Fuller accepted a position with the Woolwich Building Society, the house-mortgage firm he henceforth remained associated with, excluding wartime service. The year 1939 was notable for Fuller the artist as well, seeing the publication of his first volume of verse, *Poems.*

Perhaps we may pause for a moment in our brief biography to acknowledge that Fuller is obviously a man of great energy and discipline, combining as he did two successful careers, for on the legal side he rose to become chief solicitor of the Woolwich and, upon retirement, a member of the board, while on the literary side he published more than a dozen books of poetry, eight novels, three children's books, innumerable reviews and articles and, eventually, the two volumes of his Oxford lectures. For much of his life it was Fuller's practice to rise early in the morning to write (generally to a background of classical music) before beginning his full day's duties in the corporate world. One gathers that, given another opportunity, Fuller would not live his life in precisely the same manner. When interviewer Peter Firchow asked him if he had any regrets about his dual career, he replied:

Yes, by and large. Because I've never had enough time for writing. Also I think I could have made my mark in a different field. I've always been rather too good a lawyer to let the law languish and allow me to concentrate on my other side. I've really worked hard as a lawyer all my life and, looking back, I see that I haven't had enough time. I think it was not too bad when I just wrote verse, but I had always wanted to write prose fiction, and after the war I embarked on it in a serious way. . . . That was when the difficulties really started. To write poetry and prose and be a full-time lawyer all at once is too difficult.[6]

Fuller was called up in 1941 and he joined the Royal Navy— "thinking woollily that any hostilities in which I might be involved would be conducted at a genteel distance"—seizing when the chance arose, the opportunity to be among the first technicians trained to handle the exciting new apparatus, radar.[7] That mathematics had always been his top subject at school was a factor in this choice. In 1942 he was posted to East Africa and spent much of the next two years in Nairobi, Kenya. From the artistic viewpoint these were good years, since his duties as a radar mechanic left him ample time for writing. It was while he was serving in Kenya that his second volume of verse, *The Middle of a War,* was published and brought him his first real critical recognition. Fuller recalls, "When the clippings reached Nairobi of the reviews by Desmond MacCarthy and Stephen Spender of *The Middle of a War* in the heavy Sundays I was incredulous as well as childishly excited."[8] The poetry actually written in Africa appeared in *A Lost Season* in 1944, by which time Fuller had returned to England as a lieutenant R.N.V.R. and a desk at the Admiralty as the technical assistant to the director of Naval Air Radio.

In the closing stages of the war Fuller found the times unpropitious for poetry and turned to fiction, the genre which years previous had first engaged his creative energies but in which he had never produced work to his own satisfaction. Apprehensive about plunging directly into adult fiction, he elected to try his hand at the relatively easier task of a boy's adventure story and the result, published in 1946, was *Savage Gold,* a tale which exploited his knowledge of African native life and landscape. The war ended, Fuller returned to his duties at the Woolwich and wrote a second adventure story of crime detection, *With My Little Eye.* A fourth book of poetry, *Epitaphs and Occasions,* was published in 1949. No further books were published for three years, a period which constitutes the only significant lull in a career spanning more than forty years. One can reasonably surmise that Fuller was reestablishing his civilian life and experiencing an artistic stock-taking period, for this hiatus provides a demarcation line between the two major phases of his writing career. In 1952 Fuller was forty and his best work was still to come.

The next two decades proved fertile for both poetry and fiction, the work coming in the late fifties and early sixties including, on the whole, his finest writing. As a transition between juvenile fiction and adult fiction, he wrote two novels of pursuit, *The Second Curtain* (1953) and *Fantasy and Fugue* (1954). Thereafter he wrote six novels, *Image of a Society* (1956), *The Ruined Boys* (1959), *The Father's Comedy* (1961), *The Perfect Fool* (1963), *My Child, My Sister* (1965), and *The Carnal Island* (1970), as well as a story for younger children, *Catspaw* (1966). In more or less alternate years Fuller published six volumes of poetry, *Counterparts* (1954), *Brutus's Orchard* (1957), *Buff* (1965), *New Poems* (1968), *Tiny Tears* (1973), and *From the Joke Shop* (1975). In 1962, *Collected Poems 1936-1961* was published and included a final section of then recent but unpublished poems.

Retirement from the Woolwich in 1968 proved a relative matter, for Fuller joined the firm's board of directors, became a governor of the BBC, and was elected professor of poetry at Oxford for a five-year term. As a consequence of this election he was invited to speak at several British universities and this in turn led to a speaking tour of several Canadian universities. Fuller's Oxford lectures appeared in two volumes, *Owls and Artificers* in 1971 and *Professors and Gods* in 1973. During all of these years he was sustaining a steady flow of literary journalism, reviews, and essays for many of England's leading weeklies and monthlies. His claim that he has eased up in recent years owing to poorish health, attributable to an "officious gland," must be taken with some reservation.[9]

II   *The Two Periods*

Time will likely confirm Roy Fuller's literary significance as the postwar writer "who forms the bridge between the poets of the thirties, particularly W. H. Auden, and those of the fifties."[10] Artistically incubated in the thirties, Fuller emerged in the forties and proved a forerunner of the poetry which dominated in the fifties and was collectively known as "the Movement." He has shown remarkable staying power and a continuous capacity for steady if never striking development. At least one critic has noted the similarity between his career, on the whole a progressive one, and that of W. B. Yeats.[11]

Fuller developed slowly—he speaks of his "snail-like progress"—and accounts for this by his provincial life and his lack of university education.[12] Being largely on his own as a novice writer he wandered into "a number of more or less unsuitable influences: G. K. Chesterton, H. G. Wells, Humbert Wolfe, Aldous Huxley, *et al.*"[13] Though he began to write when he was thirteen or fourteen—"minuscule Maeterlinckian plays"—Fuller was close to twenty before he "wrote anything in the smallest degree satisfactory."[14] By then he had found congenial models and fruitful stimulation. First by the anti-bourgeois force of newly minted Pound and Eliot and then by the Marxist impulse of Auden and Spender. He recalls, "at 16 I bought Ezra Pound's *Selected Poems,* then just published, edited and introduced by T. S. Eliot. And I knew the Eliot collected poems of 1925."[15] His coming to the modernist movement when he did Fuller terms "lucky" because "it had ceased to be a mere metropolitan secret" but not yet "become academic or historical . . . ."[16] Fuller recalls, when he was eighteen or nineteen, meeting the critic John Davenport shortly after he had helped to edit *Cambridge Poetry 1929* and through him having his attention drawn to Auden, and to Spender who, according to Davenport, "had not yet published a book but who was going to be good. . . ."[17]

In various personal remarks made during the course of his Oxford lectures Fuller acknowledged debts to several poets he read in the thirties— Kenneth Allott, Bernard Spencer, Norman Cameron, Robert Graves, and Edgell Ricksworth: but elsewhere he states his "great influence has been Auden."[18] What he first received was stimulation: "In one's youth the poetry of one's exact contemporaries is exciting in an almost indefinable way— tone of voice, revelations, shared problems posed and solved. This excitement is what I got first. . . ."[19]

Without discounting the impact of Auden and Spender on the emergent consciousness of Fuller it is necessary to establish qualifications, for Fuller's debt to Auden, virtually a cliché with reviewers of his poetry, has been assumed too readily and too simplistically. George Woodcock, himself a publishing poet in the thirties, reminds us of crucial distinctions between the various circles of thirties writers. Woodcock was "loosely associated with Julian Symons' magazine *Twentieth Century Verse*" along with Fuller, Ruthven Todd, Herbert Mallalien, Derek Savage, and Keidrych Rhys.[20] He explains that this group

differed from the Spender-Lewis-Auden-MacNeice constellation in the fact that none of us had attended universities, nor did we share their country-rectory, country-house background. They were rebels from within an establishment in which we had no footing. We were lower-middle-class intellectuals, largely autodidactic, and ... we were pecu-liarily English in our approach, in the sense that we gained our sustenance from the British tradition down to Hopkins and were mostly ignorant of contemporary American poetry, with the exception of Eliot and Pound.[21]

Fuller himself has remarked on class distinction in this regard: "It's something people find very difficult to grasp about the so-called public school communists of the thirties, the Audens and Spenders and Day Lewises: one looked down one's nose very much at them. They were not thought to be proper communists at all. It wasn't simply a matter of dissociating oneself but just a feeling that one was entirely different."[22]

Aspects of thirties poetry marked Fuller permanently, primarily a belief in Marxist socialism. He says he was "brought up to believe that poetry should try to widen its audience" that it should not "address itself to a clique."[23] From this time he formulated a determination to write verse disciplined and clear, well anchored in the real world, founded on a materialistic conception of history. It is not difficult to find in Fuller's early collections expressions and images almost embarrassingly Audenesque; but to place this in perspective it is well to recall the general pervasiveness of early Auden. A veteran of the thirties, Julian Symons, has said,

Without [Auden's] stylistic example all of the young poets in that time would have written differently, some might not have written at all. The influence of Auden even upon Stephen Spender and Louis MacNeice, apart from Auden the best poets of the decade (considering it strictly as a decade, without reference to what came after), was very considera-ble, and upon most other poets it was immense. . . . Auden is where you start from, where you should start from. Spirit of Auden is the glue that makes this English poetic decade cohere, gives it shape and meaning.[24]

What is important is that awareness of these initial emulations not deflect a recognition of Fuller's particular individuality. Actually Fuller drew from only one side of Auden: "what he takes from the older poet he takes from the rational, civilized, well-ordered side of him. . . ."[25] What marks Fuller finally is a much more personal "sharply autobiographical" vein which is decidely more buttonholing than the frequently aloof Auden. [26] This quality, just as much as the public attitudes and stylistic qualities which link him with Auden and other, Audenesque writers, was to mark his poetry, through all its vicissitudes, right down to the present, so that reading Fuller's poetic oeuvre is a process of getting to know the man through the times he lives in, and the times he lives in through the man. In this he is perhaps nearest MacNiece, especially in *Autumn Journal.* And his wartime experience was doubtless a critical factor contributing to Fuller's discovery of his own authentic poetic voice, and his emergence as a recognized and significant poet. Fuller rightly adjudges that "with the coming of the long-anticipated war" his poetry "certainly improved."[27] And Ian Hamilton believes Fuller struck his distinctiveness in the process of accommodating "personal suffering" to the "public, admonitory manner of the thirties."[28] It was with *The Middle of a War* in 1942 that the characteristic stance of his work really coalesesced: "A sense of holding out against impending chaos . . . a kind of egalitarian aestheticism, rich in idealism and defeat." [29] I shall return to this shortly.

Fuller's first three volumes of poetry readily suggest he did not have to search for subject matter, this being readily provided by the concern with approaching war and its inevitable impact upon individual life, followed by the bombs falling into London, his service training, duty in Africa, and so forth. In a sense his role as poet until the end of the war was passive or reactive. He recalls, "In the Navy it often seemed sufficient just to get the observations down."[30] Thus we turn with special interest to his postwar work, curious to see what concerns he stakes out in newly austere England. Whatever the reasons for the five-year poetic lapse between *A Lost Season* of 1944 and *Epitaphs and*

Occasions of 1949—the return to civilian life, perhaps, or the writing of fiction—one is bound to sense that the poet was also undergoing a period of readjustment as far as the themes for his poetry were concerned. Indeed, Fuller has indicated as much in revealing "the personal difficulty" he had "in trying to make poetry again out of civilian life—difficulties that had already appeared when in the Navy I had exchanged a seat in the Petty Officers' Mess for a chair at the Admiralty."[31] *Epitaphs and Occasions* is not on the whole a strong volume and accordingly takes on the appearance of a transitional work between the earlier and the subsequent poetry. Another five years passed before the appearance of *Counterparts* (1954), a volume of striking assurance which announces Fuller has gained his second poetic wind, in fact has found his individual voice as never before. John Press, commenting on this period, has concluded: "Fuller is one of the most versatile and resourceful of post-war poets, a commentator on a wide variety of subjects, who enjoys ranging over an enormous field of interests."[32]

Fuller's rejuvenation proved a forerunner of things to come, for the principal historical fact of postwar British poetry is the more or less simultaneous emergence of several poets who were christened corporately "the Movement." The members included Philip Larkin, Kingsley Amis, John Wain, Donald Davie, D. J. Enright, Elizabeth Jennings, Thom Gunn, and John Holloway. These are the poets Robert Conquest included in his anthology *New Lines* in 1956. In 1963 Conquest brought out a sequel anthology, *New Lines II*, and this time included work by Roy Fuller. This was only proper since Fuller was really a father figure of the Movement, writing earlier the very type of verse which these Movement poets called for and themselves undertook to create. Fuller, who decried the low quality of work written and praised in the immediate postwar years, welcomed the Movement, with its avowed dedication to standards, enthusiastically. "During the immediate post-war decline, I certainly urged a return to Grigsonian standards of skill in versification, the purging of sentimentalism and poeticisms, a common sense of content. And in due time all this was fulfilled by the best of the poets who had been born in the twenties."[33]

The Movement poets were reacting in part against the kind of experimentation associated with Pound and with Dylan Thomas and opposed "the ambitious emotional gesture and large subject."[34] The anonymous reviewer who first employed the designation "the Movement," in the 1 October 1954 issue of *Spectator,* spoke of it as "anti-phoney . . . sceptical, robust, ironic, prepared to be as comfortable as possible in a wicked, commercial threatened world. . . ."[35] Aesthetically these poets wanted the poem to be a clear, honest "instrument for the rational control of feeling."[36] Robert Conquest, in the introductory remarks to *New Lines,* cites George Orwell as the most influential figure because of his verbal clarity and ideological independence. David Timms sees the Movement "in its formal strength and clarity of statement [as] a return to the practice of Robert Graves and the school of Auden. . . ."[37] This, of course, is the drum beat to which Fuller had marched throughout the forties. For all of these poets, regular meter and strict stanza forms were favored to insure a balance between the motives put into the poem and the emotions displayed. Advocates of the poetry hailed it as a return to the central tradition of British verse; detractors summed it up as unambitious and comfortably genteel. Present views of British poetry make perfectly clear that these contrasting views continue.

As he has been associated with the Auden of the thirties, so too Fuller has been merged with the Movement; but in both instances it is important to discern Fuller's own pattern whatever the general coloration of his setting. So far as the Movement is concerned Fuller is properly viewed as an associate member. For one thing, his treatment of erotic relationships is less domesticated, so his "wryness is more romantic."[38] Actually, his whole outlook is more expansive than that of other Movement poets. Fuller, who admits to a sense of déjà vu during the latter fifties, set about broadening his technical range, turning increasingly to syllabic verse. He says, "My own reaction to the dominant mode of the fifties . . . was on the one hand to set myself harder problems in the traditional field and on the other to try to move beyond domesticity through fictional situations, and historical and mythological subjects."[39]

Most immediately a product of the thirties, in the Wordsworthian tradition of man speaking to men, a disciple of the Arnoldian belief in poetry as a criticism of life, Fuller stands forth, with a lengthy career as testament, as one who, whatever characteristics he momentarily shared with others, was always finally his own man.

III   *The Basic Persona*

It will facilitate the process of characterizing and defining the poetry of Roy Fuller if two broad and contrasting kinds of poetry as it affects readers are brought to mind. With one order the reader is taken out of himself into ways of seeing and feeling which are unusual or unique for him. With the other order the reader is taken into himself, the poetry realizing for him what he recognizes as largely his own unformulated experience. Fuller's is a rather pure instance of this second kind of poetry. Perhaps no British poet of recent memory is more typical or representative of a normative, thoughtful, self-aware citizen. This is something of what Stephen Spender identifies in his suggestion of a decade ago that Fuller "in his poems, and as a poet, in some way provides a norm against whom other poets of the past thirty years may be judged."[40] The long-standing belief that good minor poetry reveals more about an age than the age's major poetry receives ample verification in Fuller's work. Spender believes Fuller views himself in his poetry as "an ordinary decent human being who has been thrown into a rotten kind of history and who goes round looking for a better society, occasionally hoping it will come, occasionally despairing of it."[41] Another critic makes essentially the same point in observing "that much more than the famous Three of the Thirties, Auden, Spender and Day Lewis, he is the English social poet of his period."[42] And a third critic notes that Fuller's "post-war poetry has generally been that of a quiet, contemplative family man, who uses trivial happenings of domestic existence as a starting point for an analysis of the larger horrors of modern life. "[43] The pervasive viewpoint, the critic suggests, is "suburban," and hence highly representative of contemporary life.

What is central to this work is the presence of the poet; what makes the poetry "deeply interesting," remarks Spender, is the "subdued self-portrait painted in very low tones."[44] Understatement, irony, wry wit, are everywhere employed by the temperate, often self-deprecating poet. Fuller is *the* ruminative moral poet of his time who worries his way through to small triumphs of understanding and conviction of man's essential worth.

In reviewing the *Collected Poems*, Spender astutely remarked that if they "have a single theme it is the autobiographical development of Roy Fuller who thinks of himself as *'l'homme moyen sensuel'* and as a poet just because of this."[45] George Woodcock has also commented on the autobiographical bias of Fuller's work: "His poetry can be seen as the autobiography— intellectual growing into spiritual—of a man who seeks, as he said, 'always the human in reality.'"[46] Valentine Cunningham sums all of this up very neatly in his characterization of the poetry,

The poet presents himself as the anti-hero most common to our time and place. He's not at all a man of action; his adventures are reduced to "Visiting Plymouth for the BBC" and pottering in the garden. With him and his like there's to be no more sailing from Plymouth for the azure Spanish main, instead only a negotiating of the trickier waves of azure jeans in Debenham & Freebody's.[47]

The autobiographical interpretation of this work, however, calls for considerable tact on two counts. First, the representative nature of the poetry's resident consciousness must take precedence. Fuller does not write confessional poetry. Fuller himself has made the observation that as artists grow older "their personal experiences are less varied, and therefore they are inclined to assume *personae* which don't really properly belong to them."[48] And, true enough, as his own career has advanced Fuller has inhabited various personae, though even these few exceptions prove to be simply variations on the central personage of the poems. One can read all of this verse and never doubt one's continuing contact with the same modest, gentlemanly, intelligent, calm, sometimes guiltridden, often witty individual.

The second point has to do with the speaker's age. The autobiographical development is by no means marked by a sense of passing years. On the whole Fuller appears to exist in a permanent middle age. Circumstances in the late thirties and the forties, when Fuller was younger, may be said to have aged him rapidly, world tragedy bestowing an early wisdom. This particular perspective of middle age, where awareness and caution maintain an uneasy conjunction, obviously affords rich tensions and certainly underwrites the brooding bent of the poetry.

All of this makes it evident enough that one does not find in this poetry "the wilder passions" or the "overtly lyrical," but, if this be counted something of a loss, returns flow from the quality of concern for the life experienced by thoughtful individuals.[49] Fuller, answering perhaps the charge that his verse is not sufficiently ambitious, slyly notes that he has devoted most of his poetic life "to the virtue of keeping one's powder dry rather than trying to fire the big guns."[50] A modest aim, one might say, yet one not to be underestimated or undervalued, this maintenance of quiet integrity in a noisy world.

CHAPTER 2

Early Poetry

R OY Fuller came to national prominence as a poet with his second and third volumes, *The Middle of a War* (1942) and *A Lost Season* (1944). The latter work is a sequel, for it continues the poet's chronological record of his World War II experiences commenced in the former. Taken together, these volumes constitute England's principal poetic achievement of the period. If Fuller had produced no additional poetry he would remain a significant figure, and doubtless had he suffered the fate of fellow serving poets such as Keith Douglas and Alun Lewis he would also be a romantic one by now. However, as with the early work of any continuously productive writer, these volumes are of particular interest as a prelude to the subsequent.

Fuller's first volume, *Poems,* is his only book which can be termed apprentice work, for the succeeding volumes display a writer in control of his craft. The fourth volume, *Epitaphs and Occasions* (1949), is in a special sense another first book. The author of the initial three books is not a "free" man, since he is so caught up in impending war and then the conflict itself. As a captive poet, he deals with the issues pressing immediately in upon him. So *Epitaphs and Occasions* is his first report on independence. An air of tentativeness characterizes the book, and on the whole the wartime work overshadows it. Nevertheless, the volume properly belongs to and concludes the first poetic phase. Further, there is a five-year break between its publication and the appearance of *Counterparts,* and this provides a natural line of demarcation.

I Poems

Bookseller William Caton's Fortune Press brought out Roy Fuller's first collection, *Poems,* in 1939. To say the least this is the

blandest title of any Fuller collection, for henceforth his volumes
carried pithy descriptive ones; yet "Poems" is apt enough given
the heterogeneous nature of the verse, pulling as it does in two
distinct directions. On the whole the best as well as most of the
verse is a composite of thirties themes and idiom, and it is thus
not surprising that critics have tended to attend to only these
particular poems, since they appear retrospectively to be the
groundwork of the subsequent poetry. One can quote almost at
random to illustrate the representative thirties mood and
imagery, the topography malignantly alive, threatening:

> Far off the quinsied Brenner
> The open hungry jaw
> Of Breslau and Vienna
> Through day-old papers join
> The mood of tooth and claw. . . .
>
> ("August 1936")

> Dover with pursed up lips
> Behind the purple land
> Blowing her little ships
> To danger, large and bland. . . .
>
> ("August 1938")

Accordingly, the dominant notes of *Poems* is fear. The poems
are filled with any uneasy awareness of the ominous and
tightened with anticipation of violence. This is the ambience
made famous by Graham Greene in such thirties entertainments
as *This Gun for Hire* and *Ministry of Fear.* The shadowy
protagonist of "The Journey" says, "I am like a man in an ancient
ballad/Drawn to the strangest doom."

This sense of foreboding is most strikingly realized in the
volume's most impressive poem, "To My Brother." The speaker,
alone in a London room, awaiting the imminent outbreak of war,
has apparently been reading Pope in a volume given him by his
brother who is presently somewhere in Europe. But neither
warm thoughts of his brother nor the verse of Pope, he says "can
save me/Tonight from the scenic railway journey over/Europe to
locate my future grave. . . ." Though tense with the strain of
awaiting the anticipated destruction of present culture, he
asserts his belief in the civilized values represented by Pope, and
finds solace in recollecting both Pope's loyalty to his friends and

his designation as enemies of those who "In opposition to civilisation act." The poem's most touching moment occurs with the speaker's sense of Pope's own need for reassurance, for reaffirmation of the salvation inherent in the creative imagination. A mirror into which he imagines Pope peering answers back, "you have power/First to arrange a world and then to abstract/Its final communication. . . ." This is, of course, the act of the poem itself, and the culminating communication extrapolated by the speaker comes in the fine line, "The centre land mass breathes a tragic wind." "To My Brother" anticipates Fuller's wartime poetry in several ways. The strategy of counterpointing is basic and employed in multiple ways: the general is balanced by the specific—"the perishing of the true . . . in cities" by "The Globe edition of Pope . . . open on the chair arm"; the past by the present—Pope and his grotto by "hooters from the Thames"; intellectual conceptions by physical response—the devotion to civilized principles by "The fear of living in the body." This meshing of disparate elements gives the poem its rich density and troubled suggestiveness. The aspects of language stand out. First, the imagery, sparsley employed, evokes violence and dislocation. For example, "A pistol is cocked" and "The window explodes. . . ." Second, the syntax is deliberately strained to reinforce the inherent tension of the situation: "Soldiers with labial sores, a yellowish stone/Built round the common into cubes. . . ." Moving constantly between the general, taut with straining chaos, and the personal, vulnerable but stayed by faith, the poem builds and forcefully sustains the sense of anxiety which always inhabits the living moment. The already nervous speaker, his natural uncertainty compounded by a world registering the first tremors of upheaval, can only, and justly, ask, "is it/Here we start or end?"

Many aspects of the volume testify to its origins in the times. *Derigueur* socialist feelings find expression in "Ballad of the Lost Heir," and there is the mandatory Spanish Civil War poem, "To M. S., Killed in Spain." What is to become a characteristic note of guilt is expressed by the speaker who remained behind in England: "And my existence must/Finish through your trauma. . . ." This sense of the relationship between the corporate act and the creative process, the fertilizing impact of guilt really, is brought out in the final and best stanza:

> So from the nightmare, from
> The death, the war of ghosts,
> Those chosen to go unharmed
> May join the tall city, the swan
> Of changing thoughts
> Set sailing by the doomed.

If certain images make us think of Yeats they at least reflect the truth that from the beginning Fuller has been conscious of the vital connection between the imagination and "the rag and bone shop of the heart."

That *Poems* contains a high proportion of typical thirties verse is not surprising; what is therefore especially interesting is a small group of poems which are atypical. These poems most readily bring to mind the early verse of Robert Graves. The opening stanzas of "The Journey" for example, suggest both Gravesian landscape and situation:

> Torrid blossoms of snow lay on the trees
>   Rooks courted in the hollow
> The light came like a mirror's flash
>   From even ploughed and fallow.
>
> He's travelled all day to reach that place
>   The house of local stone
> Below the line of conifers
>   That shadowed it like a spine.

The very titles imply the influence of Graves: "Centaurs," "Death," "The Pure Poet." Here are the closing lines of the last named poem in which the speaker has had a strange encounter:

> Further I could not follow him, among
> The obscure allusions to important dung,
> Nor as at length he tried a final scare
> And vanished through the non-existent door.

One is tempted to spectulate that the mysterious figure here is no less than Graves himself ("He spoke of poetry ... He said that since the Greeks few had the gifts ..."). These are items on the edge of allegory, detached from reality, and touched by the numinous. Except in perhaps the later "Mythological Sonnets," the Gravesian note is never again registered so fully; but the exotic element in the African poems, a periodic mandarin antisocial stance, and an occasional puckishness bear witness to a continuing tincture of Graves.

The student of Fuller will especially welcome these poems. They too, like most of *Poems,* may be derivative, but they do establish that the Audenesque was not the only force Fuller registered and imply an eclectic openness on his part. They force us, all to the good, not to account for later Fuller too readily or too simplistically.

II The Middle of a War

Fuller achieved his first widespread recognition with *The Middle of a War* in 1942. Highly autobiographical, the volume is arranged chronologically: the earlier poems record the responses of a civilian enduring blitz-torn London; the speaker then becomes a naval recruit undergoing basic training; an officer awaiting embarkation; finally, a member of an outward-bound Atlantic convoy. The sense of time passing is punctuated by a series of poems with the kind of title much favored at this time by Fuller such as "Summer 1940" and "Autumn 1949."

An English critic has said the volume "is probably the truest account we have of the war as it affected most people, the civilians and the majority of combatants who saw little action . . ."[1] Charting the progress of a state of mind responding to the increasing intensification of war's "enormous lust for division" ("Epitaph on a Bombing Victim"), it reflects "the individual's struggle to reconcile himself to immersion in the mass."[2] The registering of an altering sense of what constitutes reality marks one form of progression. In the opening poem, "Autumn 1939," set in the interval between the declaration of war and the downpour of bombs, the speaker can still assert, "I have no doubt that night is real which creeps/Over the concrete, that murder is fantasy. . . ." But by the close reality has shifted, as shown by the protagonist of "The Dream" whose dream of his "child's face, all bloody" prompts him to observe that terrifying life,

> allows the happy past
> To hide in that distorting mind
> Where sleep alone
> Can make it realler than the world-blown wind.

In an existence where people "race their daily ghost/In the
projectile of violent change" ("Summer 1940"), inevitably the
personal world shrinks; in "The Growth of Crime" a voice
addresses a sailor in bed with a whore:

> Each one has only his little world
> Of sensuousness and memory,
> And endeavors with the ghastly shell,
> The savage skin, the cruel eye,
> To save it. . . .

These poems are inhabited by ghosts who serve various
thematic ends: sometimes they evoke the past; are phantoms
aroused by separation; or, as in "Illness of Love," are simply the
state of actuality: "Only my fear is real and ghostly go/The bed,
the chair, the clothes and all the rest. . . ." The ghosts of "Royal
Naval Air Station" have "made uneasy every bed." It is in the
volume's most substantial poem, "To My Wife," that ghosts have
their star turn. Awakened in the night by the "voice of sirens,"
the speaker addresses thoughts to his wife who has left London
to escape the blitz. Earlier in the evening, while walking in the
park, he sees "The long pale legs on benches in the dark" and
experiences the desire of lust "as precise and fierce as that of/
The wedge-headed jaguar or the travelling Flaubert." He also
encounters two of the suburb's ghosts who represent both the
fate he and his wife have escaped and their possible destiny. "Big
Head" is deformed and so implies the luck they have had; the
"Witch," little more than a skeleton, is a disturbing image of age
who cries, *"you will come to this"* which is, ironically, a cheering
message given the present terror of obliteration by bombing.
Physical desire and a dual evocation of ghosts join in the closing
lines notable for the force of their forthrightness:

> I try to say that love is more solid than
> Our bodies, but I only want you here.
> *I know they created love and that the rest*
> *Is ghosts; war murders love*—I really say
> But dare I write it to you who have said it
> Always and have no consolation from the ghosts?

We also learn that lovers in wartime suffer not only through
separation but from the "distorting mind" as well. As the lovers
say their farewells in a great train station in "The End of a

Leave" the process of forced estrangement is already at work: "Sharp-nailed, sinewed, slight,/I meet that alien thing/Your hand. ..." Several poems touch upon the particular vulnerability of the poet confronted by war. The immensity and barbarousness of it can erode the artist's confidence and raise doubts about poetry's efficacy in confrontation with "A billion tons of broken glass and rubble." In "Soliloquy in an Air Raid," the artist expresses his fear:

> The verse that was the speech of observation —
> Jonson's cartoon of the infant bourgeoisie,
> Shakespeare's immense assertion that man alone
> Is almost the equal of his environment,
> The Chinese wall of class round Pope, the Romantic
> Denunciation of origin and mould —
> Is sunk in the throat. . . .

Like a lonely spectator watching a drama unfold in a darkened theater, the poet now "mumbles to himself" and, since he is a participant in the times and therefore open to corruption, wonders if he can "still retain the tones of civilization?" The natural limitations that flesh is heir to can also inhibit the creation of poetry as "Illness of Love" indicates. When one's very life is threatened art can seem "irrelevant" and the creative act "a waste of breath." The poet's response to the mechanical fatefulness of war is most effectively realised in "War Poet," which amplifies the sterility of his situation through paradoxical counterpointing with the newly evaluated grotesqueries of earlier poets:

> Swift had pains in his head
> Johnson dying in bed
> Tapped the dropsy himself.
> Blake saw a flea and an elf.
> Tennyson could hear the shriek
> Of a bat. Pope was a freak,
> Emily Dickinson stayed
> Indoors for a decade.
> Water inflated the belly
> Of Hart Crane, and of Shelley.

The poem continues its catalog in this vein, employing rhyme with emphatic effectiveness; then at the close, through a slight shift in meter, modulates to these telling lines:

> I envy not only their talents
> And fertile lack of balance
> But the appearance of choice
> In their sad and fatal voice.

Without discounting the authenticity of the mood at the time, we cannot help but note that the poet, like Yeats in "The Circus Animals' Desertion," makes poetry while pondering the impossibility or wisdom of doing so.

In any case, the sense of entrapment is only one facet, albeit the most important so far as quality of verse is concerned, of the poet's complex response to catastrophic circumstances; for other poems embrace a countermovement, a more hopeful strain carrying over from the thirties hopes of socialistic amelioration. In Marxist terms the war can even be viewed positively, since England, we are informed in "Summer 1940," is "realer/Today than for centuries. . ." and "the power/Is in the people to prove their collective hour. . . ." "Autumn 1940" asks, "Can we be sorry that those explosions/Which occurring in Spain and China reached us? . . ." And the reply comes back, "We see as inevitable and with relief/The smoke from shells. . ." and asserts

> . . .where the many are there is no death,
> Only a temporary expedient of sorrow
> And destruction; today the caught-up breath —
> The exaltation is promised for tomorrow.

The final affirmation of trust is in "the instinct and capacity/Of man for happiness. . . ."

Other poems bespeak the shared experiences of all soldiers. There is, for instance, the inevitable boredom common to all wars and evoked in "Defending the Harbour" through the phrase "And nothing happens," which echoes Wilfred Owen's poignantly famous "But nothing happens" from "Exposure." Similarly there is the sustained ache of servicemen cut off from their desires, as captured in "Y.M.C.A. Writing Room." The speaker, after looking at a map of the world pinned to the wall and thinking of those scattered across it, remarks, "all will carry, like a cancer, grief."

The discussion of *The Middle of a War* began by noting the dominant note of fear. It echoes to the last in the closing poem, "Troopship." The poet outward bound on the "broken sea" for duty in Africa encounters more ghosts, the "sires and grandsires" of the English aboard the troopship. These ghosts, recalling their earlier experiences, are far from consoling: "We passed this way, with good defended ill./Out virtue perished, evil is prince there still." Grim thought, but not inappropriate for those traversing submarine-infested waters in the middle of a war.

III   A Lost Season

A Lost Season (1944) continues the autobiographical chronology of *The Middle of a War*. The previous volume concluded with the poet aboard a convoy vessel. The opening poem here is "In Africa" where most of the poems are set, presumably Kenya where Fuller served, though no identifying place-names are employed. The collection concludes with his return to the England of the V-weapons period.

On the whole this is a stronger volume, certainly a quieter and more contemplative one. By contrast, the harried strain of *The Middle of a War* is the more evident. Here the poet, with time to observe his new environment at leisure and with an opportunity to order his thoughts, is more probing if less emotional. The confrontation between experience and vision continues apace, but now yields richer resolutions, the locale providing a useful perspective for viewing the offstage world drama.

The poems arrange themselves into fairly well-defined groups, so we can speak of the Africa poems, the service poems, the stock-taking poems, and so forth. About a third of the poems are specifically African and show Fuller, obviously stimulated by the exotic new world he has entered, responding to indigenous flora and fauna with obvious enthusiasm. More typically, he speculates about the alternate way of life of the native tribal civilization. He is deeply troubled by the inevitable erosion of the older culture, infection from the interloping new ones already visibly at work. In "The Green Hills of Africa," he observes,

> The prisoner proceeds by tiny doses,
> The victim weaker and weaker but uncomplaining.
> Soon they will only dance for money, will
> Discover more and more things can be sold.

The special bitterness of this, the poem concludes, is that the disease is emanating from "a world already/Dying. . . ." "The

Tribes" catalogs grotesque and cruel practices from the native
past as a way of establishing that so-called modern civilization
represents, if anything, a decline:

> The most horrible things you can imagine are
> Happening in the towns and the most senseless:
> There are no kings or poison,
> Are laws but no more reason.

The speaker also recognizes an affinity between this ancient land
and the subterranean layer of primitivism within. "The Plains"
describes how, driving at night, he catches in his headlights a
hunting lion "purposeful and unapproachable!" and thinks

> This awful ceremony of the doomed, unknown
> And innocent victim has its replicas
> Embedded in our memories and in
> Our history. The archetypal myths
> Stirred in my mind.

Fuller finds no rapport between man and the natural world.
Discussing these poems, John Press recalls Aldous Huxley's
argument that no individual who has lived in the tropics is likely
to entertain any Wordsworthian conception of man and nature
sharing spiritual union.[3] The animals are aloof and Fuller finds a
particularly apt image of this in "The Giraffes":

> So as they put more ground between us I
> Saw evidence that these were animals
> With no desire for intercourse, or no
> Capacity.

Man looking to the animals for explanatory signposts into
labyrinthine life will look in vain

> For what can be explained? The animals
> Are what you make of them, are words, are visions,
> And really they are moving in dimensions
> Impertinent for us to use or watch at all.
>
> ("October 1942")

The most impressive group of poems shows the author working
his way through to disturbing but profound truths. "Autumn

1942," "What Is Terrible," "A Wry Smile," and "Sadness,
Theory, Glass" constitute a journey into the heart of darkness.
The blackest of the poems is "Autumn 1942" because of its
radical reading of the times. In previous eras men have found
their meaning and value in action, by transfiguring the events
thrown before them by history; but now circumstances may be
such that men are corruptingly "mutilated" and all action
rendered meaningless. The choice of the human hand as the
image of something lost to the world and the oblique suggestion
of the crucified Christ combine in a troubling but forceful closing
stanza,

> It half convinces me that some great faculty,
> Like hands, has been eternally lost and all
> Our virtues now are the high and horrible
> Ones of a streaming wound which heals in evil.

The "half convinces" is characteristically Fullerian in its reserve
with this as with any other postulate. However desolate the
picture thrown up by the imagination, it will be challenged and
held at bay by the poet's deep and saving skepticism. It is this
skepticism enmeshing the other tensions in these poems that give
them their special flavor. If this tendency to undercut causes
some emotional force to seep away, it nonetheless enhances the
sense of honesty.

"What Is Terrible" opens with disturbing similies. The basic
horror of life "like cavities/Of surgery or dream" has come to
him slowly "Like the symptoms and bulletins of sickness." The
experience of being "moved across two oceans, then/Bored,
systematically and sickeningly," has pulled him sharply out of
himself. He knows now "the furious/Inner existence of objects
and even/Ourselves is largely a myth. . . ." Yet the anguish of
standing bared before the terrible "Organization of life"
prompts him to a powerful sense of community, and he sees with
new clarity that the primary values are the communal:

> I can see
> No ghosts, but only the fearful actual
> Lives of my comrades. If the empty whitish
> Horror is ever to be flushed and real,
> It must be for them and changed by them.

"A Wry Smile" sustains the sense of community as well as marking the distance the poet has come since "War Poet" of *The Middle of a War*. There he was envious of his artistic predecessors on several counts, though principally for their apparent freedom. Now he summons them to memory again, all pity spent and the shackles of self-pity broken. The assembled poets, he says, "get a quizzical ahem./They reflect time, I am the ticking." It is the great sense of unity which fosters his strength. Though "inadequate/Perhaps, and sad" he is held by the conviction that "no one/Anywhere can move, nothing occur,/ Outside my perfect knowledge or my fate."

Though not the most moving poem in the collection, "Sadness, Theory, Glass" is its thematic centerpiece and its most extended speculative probe. The speaker, seeking to come to terms with all of time, eventually discloses that the title is actually a metaphor for past, future, and present. The poem is highly representative of Fuller in staging and movement. The poet is sitting in a café over coffee at twilight looking out at a cityscape (presumably Nairobi). With his present contemplative mood he feels he "should deliver a summing-up," and proceeds to do so. He does not delude himself that a gap is inevitable between the actuality of the present and his rude rendering of it; but he suspects that with the passage of time the sense of discrepency will vanish away and eventually his "Slight poetry, like a convex mirror, hold/A cosmos, Lilliputian but exact." The future is dealt with summararily because it can exist only as "a theory." The present moment he sees as "Immense"; but though lucid, the present is actually a "distorting medium." The speaker is thus led to the conclusion that "Only the past/Is real, but it stays as sadness, like/Old age remembering sexually its youth." The moving final verse paragraph strikes a note of profound sadness. Dwarfed by massive movements of history, the poet, even in the moment of vision which allows sadness, theory, and glass to fuse, knows he "can only scribble on the margin." The closing half-dozen lines move through a sequence of cunning, unobtrusive shifts. Feeling inadequate before the seemingly insurmountable task of delivering meaningful sweeping generalizations, the poet turns to what, by implication, he can usefully manage—descriptions of representative instances of actual experience, "We saw strange southern stars revolve above/The struck ship swaying from the pointed convoy. . . ." But at the end what breaks through to assertion is the profound sense of what it is to be human, at once both deeply personal and universal, the recognition "that out of all the world/Only one other in our life would know us." This, then is the sum of the summing up.

"The Statue," the volume's most memorable poem, is built on contrasting images. The first, the equestrian statue of the title, "Distilled from some sad, endless, sordid period of time," embraces a complex of related possibilities: the aristocratic; the wilful assertion of ego; the drama of history; fine art. After developing this through five stanzas, the poem turns to the second image, clearly to be superimposed over the first, that of the face of a single man, emblematic of common humanity,

Last night between the crowded, stifling decks I watched a man,
Smoking a big curved pipe, who contemplated his great wan
And dirty feet while minute after tedious minute ran—

This in the city now, whose floor is permanent and still,
Among the news of history and sense of an obscure will,
Is all the image I can summon up, my thought's rank kill;

As though there dominated this sea's threshold and this night
Not the raised hooves, the thick snake neck, the profile and the might,
The wrought, eternal bronze, the dead protagonist, the fight,

But the unmoving, pale but living shape that drops no tears,
Ridiculous and haunting, which each epoch reappears,
And is what history is not. O love, O human fears!

Fuller has found here the right image to convey a passionate valuation of the individual life of the little man.

The subject of separated lovers, so considerable a concern in *The Middle of a War*, makes a brief reappearance. The second part of "Spring 1943" begins, "Always it is to you my thoughts return/From harrowing speculations on the age. . . ." It is his love—"Intelligent, fair and strictly moral as/A heroine of Jane's"—which balances his sense of time's chaos and underpins his aesthetic position: "No I will not believe that human art/Can fail to make reality its heart."

Though published before the end of the war, *A Lost Season* concludes on a note implying approaching victory and anticipat-

ing the return to private life. The poet turns his thoughts to this
latter in "During a Bombardment of V-Weapons," a poem which
unfolds with cunning drama. Registering the "little noises" of a
house, the tickings and drippings, the poet discovers they

> Have a power to alarm me more
> Than the ridiculous detonations
> Outside the gently coughing curtains.

But the house is simply the setting or the prelude to the crucial
drama which is to come, life with the long unlived-with wife,

> And, love, I see your pallor bears
> A far more painted threat than steel.
> Now all the permanent and real
> Furies are settling in upstairs.

A nice ambivalence results here from the presentation of
worrisome matter in nursery rhymelike manner.

Understandably, in putting down this volume one might have
taken this ominous domestic concern as a signpost to future work.
But in fact this was not the direction in which Fuller was heading.

IV   Epitaphs and Occasions

While not one of his stronger collections, considered as a
transitional book *Epitaphs and Occasions* (1949) is of special
interest in Fuller's career. Behind are the thirties and the war
with their largely self-determining subject matter; ahead is
Fuller's best work. *Epitaphs and Occasions* has about it, then,
something of the tentative and exploratory. Retrospectively we
can see that much he was to develop in the coming years is
present in this volume in a provisional way. Certain themes
insure the book's continuity with the earlier poetry—the writer's
concern with society and with his art—but there are new
interests such as the work and lives of famous artists and
geographical places associated with them; and there is a new
emphasis on matters Freudian. The poet is beginning to assume a
more middle-aged mask, one that is to become a virtual norm.
Since Fuller prefers to stand aside and observe, has a penchant
for wit and wishes to appear wise, we can understand the natural

attraction the mask of experienced age exerted.

An increase in formal neatness is perhaps appropriate in a book which begins by evoking associations with the Augustans and sustains a note which has been aptly characterized as "tart."[4] The opening poem, the volume's only lengthy one, "Dedicatory Epistle, with a book of 1949," in rhymed couplets, sets the tone for the collection and introduces several of its themes. Blending disillusion—in one critic's phrase, "political desolation"—critical bite, self-deprecation, and wit, calling into question his own conduct and that of his confreres in time past, lashing out at the wretched standards he finds in present, mean postwar England, the poet identifies what is required to restore the arts to significance.[5] He seems somewhat surprised by his own present condition and cries, "What kind of pasts must we have led/That now we're neither red nor dead?" He sees now his discontinuity from history from the start, how he and his friends

> . . . while the workless topped three million
> Read Eliot in the pavilion;
> For us the Reichstag burned to tones
> Of Bach on hand-made gramophones. . . .

He, it appears, is doubly damned: he seems as irrelevant in the present as he now realizes he was in the past:

> Alas, my talent and my way
> Of life, are useless for today.
> I might have cut a better figure
> When peace was longer, incomes bigger.
> The 'nineties would have seen me thrive,
> Dyspeptic, bookish, half-alive.
> Even between the wars I might
> With luck have written something bright.

A considerable part of what leaves him disconsolate about the contemporary scene stems from the new generation of indifferent writers:

> The younger men, not long from mother,
> Write articles about each other,
> Examining in solemn chorus,
> Ten poems or a brace of stories.

"Dedicatory Epistle" culminates in a call for a particular kind of poetry which will bring art back into touch with life:

> The poet now must put verse back
> Time and again upon the track
> That first was cut by Wordsworth when
> He said that verse was meant for men,
> And ought to speak on all occasions
> In language which has no evasions.

It is fitting that the final line of the volume, concluding "Tailpiece," sums up the poet's own resolve, "To be as truthful as reality."

The truth, the rather harsh truth, about himself and present conditions, we have already noted, is a driving motivation for many of the poems. "Meditation" strikes at certain disturbing figures currently to the fore: "raving, grubby oracles" with their books on diet and prayer and "aspirin art"; and "Mad generals" living for promotion. The poet muses further, in "The Divided Life Re-Lived," on the complacency of his own existence: "How completely we have slipped into the same old world of cod/Our companions Henry James or cats or God." But the whole truth is, of course, that life consists of more than gloom. The writer, for example, has his art in which he is "most sane, most free" ("Dedicatory Epistle"). And for all men the realm of art is compensatory.

Several titles indicate the range of Fuller's encounters with artists and their work: "On Hearing Bartok's Concerto for Orchestra," "On Seeing the Leni Riefenstahl Film," "Chekhov," "Emily Dickinson," "Poets," "Knole," and "The Lake." The lake of this latter poem is Leman, the viewing of which has prompted thoughts of Gibbon and Shelley. Looking across the water's "peacock and its turquoise," the speaker is filled with a form of hope, feeling "the lake preserved":

> For some new Gibbon's mildly-stirred repose
> In which, long after, lake-bound, he translates
> Our frightful end to ornamental prose.

A Freudian motif is at the center of a number of verses which explore the relationship between childhood experience and adult capabilities. This is given a delightful turn in "Obituary of

R. Fuller": "His infant traumas somewhat worse/He would have
written better verse. . . ." The issue of relationships is extended
to those with one's predecessors ("Ancestors"), one's father
("The Gaze"), and one's son ("Stanzas" and "To My Son"). A
sense of causality underlines these poems, and in "Image and
Fossil" the speaker as father wonders "how the son can break the
imprisoning pattern/Of cells that over generations stretch
unaltered, slattern." A related poem is "Sleeping and Waking"
wherein the dreamer, experiencing guilt-ridden dreams of such
intensity, likens himself to

> . . . an aeronaut who falls
> To worse from danger, till the drapes were drawn
> Upon the safe caged savagery of day.

Another group of poems are related by their formal compactness as, indeed, their titles suggest: "Epitaph," "Ballad,"
"Nursery Rhyme," "Song," "Little Fable," and "Hymn." These
reiterate themes already touched upon but usually with an
added dash of *accidé* of which these lines from "Nursery Rhyme"
are typical:

> Round the massive legs of man
> Scuttle all the little men,
> Busy planning for what's great
> Their own ludicrous charred fate.

The last of the occasions in *Epitaphs and Occasions* is the
presumed death of the author. This is noted in "Obituary of R.
Fuller" a humorous-serious demonstration of the hard truth
called for elsewhere in the volume. It bears some relationship to
"Sadness, Theory, Glass" of *A Lost Season* in being another
summing up. It records the life with its division between the
managerial and the poetic—"Hard to decide the more
pathetic"—his concerns, his limitations, the nature of his art. The
author of the obituary knows what of the latter is most to the
poet's credit,

> If any bit of him survives
> It will be that verse which contrives
> To speak in private symbols for
> The peaceful caught in public war.

With the benefit of hindsight I would like to speculate that underlying this poem is the author's sense of the need to die away from what he has been and an awareness of the need for a rebirth in his creativity if he is to develop. On the whole *Epitaphs and Occasions* falls below the standards of the preceding two volumes. Our reactions are likely to be mixed, mingling admiration for the sentiments with regret at the slackness and blandness of much of the verse. Retrospectively, of course, the volume can be seen as a marking of time, an instance of the poet keeping his hand in. And quite properly so since much of his finest work lay ahead.

CHAPTER 3

Middle Poetry

T AKEN as a whole the work of his middle period is Fuller's
finest and includes his most impressive single volume,
Brutus's Orchard. Much of this work creates the impression that
earlier he was holding himself in check or being overly modest in
not wanting to assert his presence. New assurance and resources
of energy come hand in hand. Dramatic situations are sought out
and exploited, and this frequently prompts a more adventuresome choice of persona. All is bodied forth in language
decidedly more vigorous and evocative.

One consequence of the ambitiousness is the creation of
several lengthy sequences, the nineteen poems of "Mythological
Sonnets," the eleven parts of "Faustian Sketches," and the
twenty-one "Meredithian Sonnets." The challenge of playing
variations on a situation obviously stimulates the poet's creative
resources.

These years, covering Fuller's mid and late forties, culminated
with the publication in 1962 of *Collected Poems*.

I Counterparts

The journey in "Rhetoric of a Journey" which begins
Counterparts is both actual and metaphoric. The time during
which the poet travels by train from his native Lancashire to
London also represents the passage of years from his
selfconscious youth to sadder, wiser middleage. As he speeds
south, away from "the dialect of love," his observation alternates
between the passing landscape and the pages of Trollope's *The
Eustace Diamonds* open on his lap, and he feels himself gaining
profounder insight into art and into the life which is both his
being and the substance of his verse. Life in the Trollope novel,
he observes, ". . . is made tolerable/ By standing away from time

45

and refusing to write/Of the hours that link the official biography." But it is these missing hours, the "something" missing from Trollope's art, which concern him. As poet he knows what he wants.

> I would like to renounce the waking rational life,
> The neat completed work, as being quite
> Absurd and cowardly; and leave to posterity
> The words on book-marks, enigmatic notes,
> Thoughts before sleep, the vague unwritten verse
> On people, on the city to which I travel.
> I would like to resolve to live fully
> In the barbarous world of sympathy and fear.

As social being he recognizes his inadequacies. His eye, for example, "Slides away from the proffered hand" and the train is taking him "to another set/Of evasions." He recognizes this forthright truth: "I can speak easily only to myself." But in fact this ratiocination crystallizes the necessary creative act, for

> ... the solemn moments of life
> Require their unbearable gaucheness translated into art.
> For the guilt of being alive must be appeased
> By the telling observation, and even feeling
> Can only be borne retrospectively.

It appears as if in the five years separating *Epitaphs and Occasions* and *Counterparts*—a period during which he wrote his first two novels—Fuller had resolved to claim new subtleties of experience for his contemplative verse. With the advantage of hindsight we can view "Rhetoric of a Journey" as a virtual manifesto for this next phase of his poetic career. The essential movement, away from "the waking rational life" into "the barbarous world" of the hidden wellsprings of life is, of course, a matter of emphasis; for Fuller had never ignored the enigma of human motivations nor does he abandon, as *Counterparts* amply illustrates, a continuing concern for the overtly political. The journey, thus, is toward, if not greater truths, then previously undisclosed or unacknowledged ones: the truth of the missing hours.

Admissions of inadequacies as a social being may be seen now as the poet's starting point. Earlier poetry had admitted his ineffectuality as a political participant and been the source of recurring guilt and desolation; but now the inadequacy in the public realm is a consequence of the private man's social limitations. This recognition, however painful, proves not to be a fresh source of guilt but rather a stimulant toward the creation of a rich inner drama of the self. Accordingly, the poems become the counterparts to failure, the vital consequence of unlived life.

To judge by "The Two Poets" Fuller is aware that the earlier self has been supplanted. The young now dead poet is being mourned by the older poet as "witty and observant" and blessed with a "lucky manner." The older poet, admitting he labors at his work, characterizes himself as one who "counted beats, weighed vowels/His verse as thick and piled as bowels." Another set of counterparts. Here and elsewhere in the volume the poet worries about his art, both as process and product. Fundamental is the question, Will my work survive? for he admits in "To a Notebook," "That's my constant care,/Living a miser for a doubtful heir."

The antithetical tensions of despair and hope, pleasure and pain provide the dramatic framework for other poems tracing the interplay between life and art. The most personally revealing of these is "Poet and Reader," done with a particularly light touch. The poem is in the tradition of A. E. Housman's "Terrance This is Stupid Stuff," since it is an apologia for the pervasive current of gloom running through the poetry. The first verse is given over to an imagined typical reader, clearly out of patience with the poet's depressing obsessions, "with years and death," who suggests that life really is not as bad as made out. The poet admits at once that his creativity "Comes out of moods of pleasure" but defends his recurring stance with the reminder that meaningful art must never blink at the basic tragedy of inevitable defeat,

> All art forsees a future,
> Save art which fails to weigh
> The sadness of the creature,
> The limit of its day,
> Its losing war with nature.

"Poem to Pay for a Pen" catches the poet, at least briefly, in an atypical sour mood,

I do not know which are the most obscene:
Poets, profoundly sceptic, scared, unread:
The leaders monolithic in their mania;
Or the unteachable mass, as good as dead.

But he ends by reaffirming the necessity and value of art "That
with the grossest means, pen, gut and brass/Resolves and then
transcends the mortal pain." So it becomes increasingly clear
that for Fuller art provides the bedrock faith. Thus his constant
worrying in his verse and criticism about its place in the world
and the tendencies which would demean or corrupt it is easy to
understand.

Two poems pay homage to admired writers. "Ibsen" admits
the ridiculousness of certain of the dramatist's surface activities,
but finds at the heart of "the foliate five/Acts" the essential
"pulsing germ." That is, the ability to break past crude
interpretations of life to the crucial and hence vitalizing truths.
"Andre Gide" extols a writer for whom Fuller obviously has
profounder feelings. Gide is virtually indispensable, since his
"practical travel notes" are essential to the following of any
route the modern intellectual may choose to "haunt." Gide
possessed the requisite attributes of the great writer. He could
resolve contradictions in his art; he was able simultaneously to
register the full "weight/Of intimate anxieties" and to project a
consoling "general hope." Because of these gifts he was able to
fulfill the artist's highest calling in the human community,

. . . by allowing smaller men to share
Such nights of his made theirs the less to bear,
Even to answer to creative need.

Before turning to the triumphs of this volume, the poems in
which Fuller best realizes his artistic ideals, we may note the
least effective work. These are generalized responses to the
times, items from which the poet in any direct way has excluded
himself. "Socialist's Song" is about the little man who both
suffers "the fate" of and is the "only support of the state." "The
Fifties" offers the pleasure which resides in any reasonable
rendering of a roundel, but its generalized gloom over yet more
wretched times is obvious and slack. By contrast "Death of a
Dictator" displays how a public event can provide a source for
effective poetry. This is actually the poet's response to the death

of Stalin, although nothing in the poem discloses this.[1] Depicted waiting amid "ugly furniture" for the passing of an oppressively tyrannical father lying upstairs are his children, their feelings mingling "poignant memories of their youth" and "hate." The poem is a miniaturized rendering in verse of a typical Ivy Compton-Burnett novel.

The more personal poems with a strong sense of persona are the real flesh and blood of *Counterparts,* particularly "The Image" and "Translation," two of Fuller's most anthologized pieces, and justly so. "Translation" is something of a bridge poem standing astride the poems still to be considered and the political ones just touched upon.

Among other things, "Translation" is a rarity in Fuller in the expression of nonguilt. As the title suggests, the work purports to be a statement about another age. But references quickly enough reveal the humorous employment of anachronism. The mandarin protagonist provides a brief but encompassing summing up of his times and therefore explains, and plainly justifies in his view, why he is going to wash his hands of them and embrace a secluded life. The first stanza sets the pattern to be repeated with elegant variations in the remaining six,

> Now that the barbarians have got as far as Picra,
> And all the new music is written in the twelve-tone scale,
> And I am anyway approaching my fortieth birthday,
> I will dissemble no longer.

His catalog of distress encompasses "quarterlies/Devoted to daring verse," the anticultural "stupidity" of the masses, "wretched wars and innumerable/Abortive revolutions," and so forth. Crucial to the poem's success is that the anger apparent in the explicit statements is not transmitted emotionally. The speaker's studied syntax and the formal neatness of the form represent his control and assertion of personal standards. Characteristic of the best Fuller verse is an unobtrusive compounding of effect, the deliberate disavowal of a simplistic response. "Translation" provides an an excellent instance of this. While Fuller doubtless has a great deal of sympathy for his protagonist's views he does not absolve him from ironic treatment. When he retires, as he indicates is his intention, to the farther side of Picra—Fuller needling himself about life in Blackheath?—what is he going to do? Why "write some poems/

About the doom of the whole boiling." That, in the terms the poem has made abundantly clear, is indeed an act of futility, to say nothing of a true abdication of the artist's responsibility.

Familial responsibility, aging, and death are the concerns of the poems of the private life. "The Image" examines the unending conflict between ruthlessness (the impulse to obliterate the unattractive or the unappealingly demanding aspects of daily life) and compassion or tolerant accommodation. A close reading of this forceful work is in order both because it is probably Fuller's best-known poem by virtue of frequent anthologizing, and because so representative of his finest work in setting, movement, economy of means, attitude, and emotional impact. "The Image" begins with a simple notation, "A spider in the bath. The image noted:/Significant maybe but surely cryptic." The second line obviously shows the mind making its initial response. There is an intuitive sense that the observation can be made to bear meaning, but the drama results from the sense of a response too casual to generate any real concern and hence engagement. Almost idly expanded description follows, "A creature motionless and rather bloated. . . ." This is preparatory and will actually be held in reserve. Now the speaker does follow through to record what is more interesting than the image, his own immediate response: "Passing concern, and pity mixed with spite." It is this last word, reserved for the stanza's climactic position, which strikes out the context of casualness with bite. It also proves an instance of foreshadowing, preparing for the specific and disturbing instance of spite at the poem's heart.

The second stanza opens by pursuing the narrative line, "Next day with some surprise one finds it there." This works in a dual manner. Clearly the primary drama stems from the return to and reopening of the issue. We sense at once that the protagonist is going to be pushed further and likely prompted to explore the implications of his ruthless stirrings. What is not immediately evident is the underlying secondary sense of how easily the whole matter could have been forgotten and unresolved but for the happenstance of the spider's seeming inertia. While any student of poetry will appreciate how difficult it is to pin down in any precise way the manner in which a complex effect is achieved, it is nevertheless important to acknowledge the fission taking place under the apparent surface. It is especially important to register this with a deceptively straightforward, seemingly explicit poet such as Fuller. A reader of his poetry will often be aware of a discrepancy between the simplicity of much of his work and the degree or effect it achieves, which suggests at once that an unobtrusive dramatic activity, easily overlooked, is taking place.

This stanza continues the pattern of the first as the mind is shown moving toward an as yet unseen destination. This drama of the process of rumination is actually the crucial art of the Fullerian poem. Here the mind makes first a minimal registration of data, "It seems to have moved an inch or two, perhaps." The "perhaps" is another earmark of this work reflecting a deeply skeptical being and artistically sustaining the immediate possibility of creative spontaneity. The mind is not assertive, remaining tentative and, significantly, open. The third line turns to humor, operating as both retardation and contrast, "It starts to take on that familiar air" — also reflecting the ease of the speaker who vis-à-vis the spider possesses complete control of the situation. The line does not, of course, complete the statement, but the break has the effect of providing the pause in which the mind seeks an appropriate metaphorical resolution. The next two lines deliver this in two stages. The momentum of the third line's lightness is sustained, but the connotation of the word "prisoners" qualifies this and sets up an appropriate transition into the surprising and disturbing fifth line. It is appropriate to see the three lines together:

> It starts to take on that familiar air
> Of prisoners for whom time is erratic:
> The filthy aunt forgotten in the attic.

The final line constitutes the most intense moment in the poem and completes its first movement. "The filthy aunt" line is unquestionably one which strikes with sudden and sharp force, cunningly led up to, and though hinted at earlier by the word "spite," nonetheless leaps into the unexpected. Perhaps it is not unreasonable to observe that we have been thrust through the whited sepulcher of the gleaming bathtub into a domestic heart of darkness. The forthrightness of the admission or confession carries force as well. Four of the seven words contribute their own particular strain to the impact.

Let us start with the word "aunt." Whatever the aunt may be assumed to represent, the essential point is that it is something

closely related to the speaker and thus involving deep responsibility. Yet the responsibility owed an "aunt" is less stringent
than even more basic familial ties. The response to an aunt
therefore becomes a meaningful barometer of compassion. It is
not needful aunts as such who prompt feelings of revulsion and
disclose a primitive desire to shuck off the aged and crippled, but
"filthy" aunts. This word is capable of releasing a multitude of
unattractive images, of physical debilities, the messes of
uncontrolled functions which we instinctively shy away from and
would prefer to avoid. If the initial response is one of shock or
disturbance, the more thoughtful secondary one will likely
recognize the deep-seated truth that most lives encompass
aspects which the individual would wish to hide away in an attic,
the burial center for private matters too painful to ever be truly
disposed of. Attic, as the place which hangs over one's head,
doubtless carries more force than basement which is more
suggestive of burial. Perhaps the word "forgotten" is at once the
most subtle and surprising of all. If we consider how the word
"hidden," for example, would operate as a replacement we begin
to suspect the richness of forgotten. First off, as the statement
shows, the aunt is *not* forgotten; and in any case the remainder of
the poem makes clear she would not be forgotten. So, in this
context, "forgotten" expresses unconscious desire, which is to say
that the word choice conveys the intrusion of instinctual, innate
antipathy. "Forgotten" thus is unconscious desire. The discrete
reverberations then of this quartet of words help account for the
rich texture of effect, the phrase "help account for" recognizing
the dimension of mystery residing in thoughtful poetry. The
remaining three stanzas may be viewed as absorbing or coming to
terms with the potency of the line we have been considering.

In stanza 3 the protagonist returns to the routine activity of
accounting for the appearance of the spider in this particular
place, and of speculating as to why it has not moved. Following
the by now apparent patterning of the stanzas, moving from the
overt to the covert, the conclusion takes on the developing
double meaning,

> the problem must be faced;
> And life go on though strange intruders stir
> Among its ordinary furniture.

While the immediate statement concerns the disposition of the
spider, the profounder meaning speaks to the problem of the

antihuman impulse. Both "problem" and "strange intruders" can refer to the aunt and what she represents, but can as well identify the irrational in its self assertion, that which entered the poem with "spite."

The fourth stanza relates how the protagonist saves the spider, slipping a piece of paper under it before putting it out the bathroom window. The description of the action lowers the tension in preparation for the emphasis of the final stanza. Even here, scaled down, the concluding word "flung" echoes the earlier force of concluding words. The last stanza explicitly brings the relationship between spider and aunt into focus to reveal an essential difference. The former can be disposed of, not the latter: "We certainly would like thus easily/To cast out of the house all suffering things." Actually this is an ambivalent statement and so adds still further to the poem's effectiveness. To put out the spider is to save it and with this self-evident truth operating the act of casting out seems logically to imply that if this action would save "all suffering things" we would perform it. But the sentence, given the context of the preceding stanzas, appears to ask us to view the casting out as a selfish act of personal sloughing off of unattractive appendages. Obviously, the statement pulls in opposite directions simultaneously. The poem itself, then, can be seen to enact with deceptive simplicity and remarkable economy the complex individual engagement with ruthlessness—the vestigal counterpart in human beings to the natural economy of the animal kingdom—and the counterassertive humane impulse.

The concluding lines constitute the final staging of the conflict and its resolution as fellow feeling asserts itself. The final lines are not a dying fall but a forceful climax made strong by irony:

> But sadness and responsibility
> For our own kind lives in the image noted:
> A half-loved creature, motionless and bloated.

The most obvious feature to register is how the closing of the penultimate line matches the second half of the opening line, while the last line is a variation of the poem's third line. This recapitulation allows us to contrast the initial meaning with the much denser significance of the closing and measure the distance traversed. The final shock of a recognition comes in seeing the spider or at least the description of it as the self. In this way the vexing question of human motivation remains obscure. Without denying the validity of human virtue, the functioning of responsibility, the statement nonetheless subtly leads us to sense that our compassion for the suffering and helpless emerges from a sense of the end toward which we ourselves are moving—the reason we truly have cause for "sadness." The casual notion of the opening comes full circle with the disturbing vision of the self as "half-loved creature," and the insight, that we save others that we may ourselves be saved. This representative analysis demonstrates, I trust, that the seeming simplicity of much of Fuller's verse is largely illusory.

A similar note sounds in "Côte des Maures" when the speaker, on holiday, is uncertain whether the sights naturally assume "The drama of unpurposed lives" or if his subjective being so colors them,

> The traveller finds waters, brings his own
> Disease. The poet's eye, impervious
> To all except his fears, gives back a world
> Dark, coloured, miniature, attractive, false.

Human frailty and response to it, authentic counterparts, are explored in other items. "Ten Memorial Poems" record the stages in the process of coming to terms with the terminal illness of an older man (actually Fuller's stepfather). The two most moving moments memorialized are those when the speaker becomes first aware of the dying man's efforts to put at ease those about him, and when, the visitation of suffering already having outstayed its welcome, despised death is fervently hoped for.

Fuller is aware of how easily modern man can fall into complacency, an unobtrusive and therefore insidious form of dehumanization. Several poems register moments when the nonhuman world strikes seemingly inadvertently at this complacency, and see this as a fortuitous thing. The protagonist of "Inaction" in enjoying his breakfast reading *The Times*—"the entertainment of the morning"—when his insulated existence is, as he interprets it, assaulted. Looking out the window he sees a strange dog appear and defecate on his car. Immediate "indignation gives way to unease." He senses the "sneering" dog's act is a comment on his life. The poem's bite comes from its sustained irony. Caught between the morning headlines and the intruding dog, the speaker will "The fate of millions take half seriously."

Four poems capture the indifferent and threatening face which nature turns to man. I noted earlier when discussing the African poems that Fuller displayed no sympathy for a Wordsworthian view of rapport existing between man and nature. "A Wet Sunday in Spring" is the most striking of these because of its potent projection of nature proliferating cancer-like and keeping the human world under constant seige,

> The ivory-horned chestnut
> Effortlessly assumes its task; the rain
> Is perpendicular and horribly fertile;
> The embattled green proliferates like cells.
> I think feebly of man's wrong organisations,
> Incurable leaders, nature lying in wait
> For weakness like an animal or germ. . . .

A winterscape in "The Snow" prompts similar feelings of man's vulnerability by evoking in the perambulating speaker archetypal memories of cold, wolves, and deep forests. "Sentimental Poem" states explicitly that nature cannot "sympathise/ Or love" and characterizes "human emblems" as "strange and frail." Finally, "Images of Autumn" considers the relationship between nature and poet. This is a double-edged affair. Because the poet is a man nature is indifferent to him—"his new interest in the world is not/Reciprocated"—but since he is a poet, nature is a source of stimulation and material (as these poems make evident). This is marked in a striking sentence, "The autumn flood/Of symbols pile behind the poet's sluices." Particularly in its autumn guise, nature becomes a counterpart to aging, decaying man. As nature fills the gutters with "thick and rustling treasure" the aging poet leaves his verses. This is an appropriate poem with which to conclude a discussion of *Counterparts*, separating out as it does poet and man as did the initial poem, "Rhetoric of a Journey," with the poet concerned about the "something" absent from Trollope's fiction and the man conscious of his social inadequacy. The volume, it is apparent, flowered from this fertile dichotomy.

II   Brutus's Orchard

One of the early sentences in *Brutus's Orchard,* from "Pictures of Winter," is, "I dig the soil and in its barren cold/Surprise a bulb-bomb fused with palest gold." Both in its richness of image and in its representative act it is emblematic of this the poet's finest collection. Fuller begins to inhabit a more dramatic and more dynamic universe and so achieves a new breadth of conception. This letting go as it were gives the poems greater force and reveals new resources of energizing verbal intensity. Speaking of this volume, Roger Garfitt states, "When the star of Fuller's 'reasonable youth' went into eclipse, he had to divine beyond reason and humanity, to the deeper springs of volition."[2]

Epitaphs and Occasions created, as noted, an ambience of the Augustan period; *Brutus's Orchard* moves farther back in time, as the title suggests, to evoke a sense of the Renaissance. Many of the book's concerns echo those of Elizabethan writing: the particular response to nature; the sensuality and the infections transient flesh is heir to; the contrariety of life and the constellations; the fecund panorama of ancient mythology. It is true that only one of the three poets alluded to, Shakespeare, represents the Renaissance, but Byron and the later Yeats share the sense of amplitude we associate with the late sixteenth century. The particular Yeats whose presence is felt is the "wicked" one filled with untrammeled admiration for womankind. The volume is dominated by the theme of sexuality which is viewed as the essential source of energy for both life and art. In a sense the buried libido proves to be the "bulb-bomb fused with palest gold."

The opening trio of poems, "Spring Song," "Summer," and "Pictures of Winter," announce at once both the major themes and the new verbal activity. Both stem from an intensified sense of antithesis operating in the world. The previous volume explored variations of counterparts; here a more radical form of pairings, opposites, provide poetic armatures. Life holds compelling mixtures of the sublime and the ridiculous, the glorious and the horrifying. It is a dangerous universe, both exhilarating and frightening, filled with bulb-bombs and "white explosions of cloud." The nature depicted in "Summer" is double-faced: on the one hand, a fabulous mother forever sending out "Fresh notions of brow and feather/To perpetuate the race"; on the other, the source of "occasional error," spawning the corrupt cells "From which the conquerors spring."

Much of the dialectical activity involves pairs or groups of poems. A striking contrast is provided by "Autobiography of a Lungworm" and "Elementary Philosophy." We see the poet open to all experience, for the former burrows deep within the organs of the swine to observe the realm of the minute worm while the latter confronts "Four thousand million years," "Planets and stars," and "endless shores." We might reasonably expect to be squeemish over the probing of a lungworm and exhilarated by the spectacle of stars. The expressed attitudes are rather the reverse. The poet communicates awed amazement at the intricate, patient existence of the worm, the eggs waiting "For years, if necessary," for "the lucky match" which will sustain their destiny. Though the poet denies the ability to fathom the significance of this incredible form of life, he senses that it demonstrates the potent capacity in creation for survival, that life "has a wiry soul/That must escape the knife." If the lungworm is actually a source of comfort, the universe writ large in "Elementary Philosophy" is otherwise, for it has "hatched . . . staggering fears," and even the buds of the current spring present intimations of "final wars." These are the poles between which man, at once awed and appalled, must maintain his existence and, hopefully, his equilibrium. Standing quite appropriately, between these two poems in the text is the four-liner "On Grazing a Finger" which brings home in routine circumstances the waring of the elements. The small wound leaves man exposed before the rampant forces of destruction; yet he knows the counterattacking forces of healing commanded by his vital body. The battle between the wounds of life and recuperative energy is ceaseless.

Several other poems exploit the contraries, ironies, and absurdities hedging life at every turn. The very fine "Eclipse," with the subtitle "January 19, 1954: 12.50-4.13," seizes upon this unusual and transient moment in the heavenly sphere as an image of man's "incredible" dreams. The time of eclipse showed the world in its true nature,

> So last night while we slept the moon
> Crawled through the shadow's long black spear,
> Finding in all that sun-ruled void
> The darkness of the human sphere.

The following evening, the occasion of seeming cataclysmic
threat past, "life and planet / Take their far stations as before."
The moon resumes its cast of utopian permanence while life,
shrinking to the image of a house, goes on "Upon the rotting
floor. . . ."

Though less resonant than "Eclipse," "Night Piece" is
argumentatively much denser. It posits a correlation between
the sensual and violent dreamworld and the cataclysmic realms
of the galaxies "indifferent to wrong." Into the daylight world
press, from dream and universe alike, only slight intimations of
chaos. On earth, "Only edges of the harm / Can protrude" while
the only hint of the universe's lethalness resides in the fate of the
moon.

> Bloody, quartered, very near,
> In a portion of the sky
> Fateful to man's destiny;

Why is it that man does not collapse in terror, trapped between
these twin madnesses beyond his control? Two explanations are
offered. First is "native human hope" which acts like a
"reversing telescope" to miniaturize the threat of extinction.
Second is "the blunt/ Instrument" the human body which is
content to extrapolate from the raging data "Merely symbols."

The impressive "The Perturbations of Uranus," though
utilizing cosmic imagery, concentrates on the libidinous impulse
and considers what it is that dissuades men from giving it free
rein. This is one of Fuller's familiar little staged dramas in a
seriocomic vein. The speaker's line of thought has been
prompted by his viewing in the café where he is seated a nubile
young waitress who has returned his stare with "A candid gaze."
A self-conscious intellectual, he registers once again "How still
the world belongs to the obtuse/ And passionate." The "learned
men" too can feel passion, but they, because not obtuse,
transmute it. The argument in part is a theory of art for "Our art
is the expression of desire," and Yeats is quoted as saying

> one who buys a landscape for
> Its beauty takes home in his arms the bare
> Outrageousness of an uncaring whore. . . .

Art actually trains us to withstand the "transcendent moments of
existence" when "the will is powerless." Lust, rather paradox-

ically, puts us in touch with the truth of ourselves, and when we
"feel brain from spare body torn," releases the powers of pity
and an awareness of the truth of "short degraded lives" which in
turn prompts artists and prophets to seek after "virtuous law and
golden hives." The poem offers a fine image to convey the
operation and disclosure of emotional forces in recollecting that
"The planet Neptune's existence was revealed / Only by the
perturbations of Uranus." The poem cunningly draws together
lust and idealism. Lust will occur "again and yet again" in the
male and though seldom fulfilled, his body will respond to the
female ever willingly. The force of this physical necessity spills
over to suggest man's potential for dreams and visions is equally
inexhaustible. Surprisingly but clearly, the sources are shared.
Once we accept that the pulsations of Uranus caress Neptune we
appreciate it could not be otherwise.

Earlier, while discussing "André Gide," I noted Fuller's
admiration for the French writer's ability to console his readers
by exposing them to uncomforting truths while never relinquish-
ing a sense of hope about the ultimate significance of existence.
Repeatedly we can see this as a primary aim of the Fuller poem.
"Discrepancies" makes the balancing act quite overt. The ten
stanzas work out a sequence of variations moving from the less
serious to, doubtless from the artist's viewpoint, the very serious,
a movement virtually from the ridiculous to the sublime. The
opening links power and inadequacy,

> Even smooth, feared executives have leisure
> To show the inadequacy of their love:
> The longest day must end
> In animal nakedness.

Typically, Fuller concludes by mingling the rather absurd
sacrifice of poets for their art and its consequences,

> The sublimation of the poets rise
> From their renunciation of the coarse hair
> And the inanities
> Of ravishing crimson lips. . . .

Contradictions dot the human drama: "Bravery out of freaks,
ethics from hate/ And valid economies/ Of starving theorists."
The thematic variations and the form itself, the movement back
and forth between the long lines and the short, underline one

certainty of what is being cataloged: its predictability.

Particular poets, the nature of art, the relationship between art and its time, and the personal life of the artist are subjects relating several poems. In "To Shakespeare" the speaker says that with advancing years he has learned the meaning of the feelings and actions of Shakespeare's protagonists. They are the "great symbols of/ The shapes that human life must take": for all human life is dramatic. Shakespeare's own simple yet "mysterious" life "within a reign of strife" knew the relationship between the private and the public and accordingly "experienced" all of which he wrote. Though the great dramatist's special powers set him apart he employed the myth which all poets must employ, namely, that life is impure and the forces of history impersonal.

Most impressive of this group is "The Final Period" because the speaker distills depths of feeling in verse Yeatsian in its dignified, compacted simplicity. He is an older poet who, seated at his desk, sees his youthful daughter on the lawn, and she, as representative of youth, womanhood, and daughter, underwrites his speculation. These provide an encompassing insight into his growth as a man, his motivations as a writer, his sense of life and of the relationship between art and experience. His words indicate that he is deeply moved and caught up in conflict between the desire to experience life intensely and the blunting knowledge of experience. "With youth's desire" he writes of life's "alarms" and of "erotic rage." He knows, however, that the forces of the buried life and the imagination flatten out in daily living. His daughter will merely "sigh" while he will quit his desk "and try/ To live with ordinary powers." And so the balancing act continues ever, wisdom transmuting the facts,

> Bermuda or Byzantium—
> To some utopia of forgiving
> And of acceptance I have come.
> But still rebellious, still living

In the wisdom of a final period he can confront all things—the personal pain of his own past failures in love, betrayals by words, human deficiency, and accept not only noons of "green and blue" but, as well, "archipelagos of dung"—so that in his art at least "all will be whole." The poem's proximity to "The Perturbations

of Uranus" can be seen when he says it is his daughter for whom
he writes, hoping to assist her through

> Her painful and tumultuous years,
> So she would awake at last in true
> Epochs, to music of the spheres.

As well as of Yeats this may also remind one of D. H. Lawrence
preaching against the conception of happiness and in favor of a
doctrine of vitalism which urges a continuous engagement with
life.

Other poems make clear the poet's ongoing arguments with
himself. The sense of power and control conveyed by "The Final
Period" is countered elsewhere by expressions of doubt about
both the self and the times. "Expostulation and Inadequate
Reply," addressed to Coleridge, has as epigraph a quotation from
one of Coleridge's letters to Wordsworth, asking the latter to
write a poem which will cheer those who, as a consequence of
the French Revolution, "have thrown up all hope of the
amelioration of mankind, and are sinking into an almost
epicurean selfishness." The poet protagonist admits the times
still require such a work, but knows he is not the man to write it.

Appropriately, the poem's chief target is the many poets of the
age "trivial or meaningless." While insisting upon his own
inability to write the requested poem, the poet nevertheless
offers a consoling belief in the generality of mankind. Slowly and
haphazardly "grand assaults" upon such "barricades" as privilege will result from a "totality of action" carried out "by many
men who each alone are blind/ To what they do, and may do."
The poem is reminiscent of the wartime work in which Fuller
felt robbed of freedom by the massive movement of history in
which he was caught up. At the close the speaker pessimistically
asserts the impossibility of pure belief; but this in turn is
countered by the implied sense that all is not lost so long as art
can know and speak of what Coleridge demanded. Given the
times, awareness is the best that is possible, but that is something.
This is the burden of the concluding lines,

> This could not be the poem you desired.
> We grow to understand that words alone,
> The visionary gleam through which the poet

More and more consciously, less frequently,
Renews his youth, are, like all art, condemned
To failure in the sense that they succeed.
You, who so early lost that power, know best
How men forever seek, not quite in vain,
Sublime societies of imagination
In worlds like this, and that no more exist.

"One and Many" reenacts another of the poet's journeys of discovery. He believes the earlier writers were able to portray individual men as unique yet natural, something the moderns are unable to do; for their figures inevitably turn into emblems of "A stringent world the artist never made." But further thought leads the poet to the recognition that the artists of both periods really share a continuity of experience. The figures depicted during the earlier period were privileged, masters with "great boots and thighs," and the speaker thinks of the masses of men in the background, the "industrious world of normal men." Recognition of the shared universality of experience is consoling however absurd the nature of that fate, "A miser body made for giving/ And which prepares for war desiring love."

Humor keeps the whole issue of poet and poetry in perspective in "Poem Out of Character." Implying that his poetry normally offers up "symbols of a comic size" and that its typical subject matter is "Ambiguous cats and sweets and birds" (all subjects having their corresponding Fullerian poem), the poet does report on the matter which inhabits his dreams and which he wishes he could make "tremendous statements" about like "great planets." The poem is purportedly atypical as well in expressing a belief in the totality of existence. This possibility exists because the poet accepts the limitation of his perception; since he looks through "tiny apertures" he can intuit that "what enures/ In truth" are "enormous joys."

"Dialogue of the Poet and His Talent" most directly states the underlying conflict of this group of poems. Both poet and talent discover they share an identical wish and an inability to fulfill it, "To be committed or to stand apart:/ Either would heal the wound." So paradoxically a healed wound would prove destructive with fructifying ambiguity dying into silence.

"At a Warwickshire Mansion" opens with ambiguity since the speaker's tensions are both "wished " and "detested," but this poem rather emphasizes the latter in its comments on art and hence counters the works which glorify it. Art "is never innocent," and the writer well aware of " the sleight of hand which points the blunt/ Compresses, lies."

Excluding the "Mythological Sonnets," the remaining poems divide themselves into those of low and those of high drama. Four short poems talk about illness and death. "The Day" marks the day, unrecognized at the time of course, which initiates the final or killing phase of one's life. It is akin to "idle Byzantium" unable to register "The presence in her remoter provinces/Of the destructive followers of the Crescent." In a similar vein, "To a Girl in the Morning" accords recognition to that unique woman in every man's life: she who is the last to prompt his lust. "On a Textbook of Surgery" draws a rather grim comparison between the horrors "colourless flesh" can suffer and the "highly-coloured" nature of these horrors. The ironically titled "Pleasure Drive" reminds one of the omnipresence of death and notes that its chances of fulfillment actually increase during a leisurely auto excursion. The "smiling" driver's road may end at any time "in blood and wrecked machine." Many of the volume's poems, and especially this quartet, are neatly summarized by a concluding statement from "Pleasure Drive":

> Even when classes do not slap each other
> And generations accept their heritage,
> In times of monolithic calm, the single
> Life must enjoy its happiness between
> Atrocious thoughts. . . .

Contributing markedly to the overall richness of this volume are two quite different but equally dramatic poems, "The Ides of March" and "Florestan to Leonora." Both could be taken as speeches from Renaissance dramas. The first is in effect a soliloquy by Brutus while waiting in his garden for the arrival of the fellow conspirators against Caesar (so the poem is the inspiration for the book's title). Though the poem doubtless glances back to Shakespeare's *Julius Caesar*, the more probable antecedent is Fuller's own earlier "Translation." In that poem an effete Roman mandarin is so distressed with his society that he decides to retire into an isolated life. "The Ides of March" is a radicalization of "Translation." That is, the speaker's situation is obviously much more dramatic and his involvement with murder a decisively direct intrusion into national politics up against the passive withdrawal of the earlier protagonist. Brutus emerges much more fully developed because the question of his motivation is crucial as it is not in the earlier instance. Another feature shared with "Translation" is the use of anacronism, so the poem is not so much an historical set piece as a fresh means of commenting on the contemporaneous as well as suggesting the continuity of history. Brutus, for example, makes reference to books and employs in a simile a box of chocolates. Brutus is a variant of the persona employed in much of Fuller's work. Basically a domestic person who engages in "a little amateur scribbling" in his garden, he hardly strikes one as a commanding figure moving in the corridors of powers. Since the protagonists in many Fuller poems bewail their ineffectuality in the public sphere it is tempting to see such a poem as this as a form of positive relief; here is someone who is actually going to act. Brutus says, "And now I am about/To cease being a fellow traveller." His motivation is really a desire to remove the guilt which burdens him as a consequence of his life of privilege. He hopes his wife will see him in the "compromising presence" of those of "simpler motives" with whom he has allied himself so she will "know that what we built had no foundation/Other than luck and my false privileged role...."

Since the criticism of society is neither new nor made with the cutting edge employed in "Translation," the real emphasis and pleasure of the poem falls upon the casting of this sensitive, overly self-conscious, nervous, somewhat fastidious man in a dangerous and vital situation. Fuller achieves his impressive effect by carrying his figure tantalizingly close to the comic without letting it actually take over. Strikingly the comedic actually enhances Brutus's dignity and sincerely felt concern. Brutus is an everyman figure in no way seeking to enhance or enlarge his position or answer the needs of his own esteem. He impresses by the very fact that in the face of his own nature he is going to fulfill a task he deems must be accomplished. A consideration of the closing portion of the soliloquy gives insight into Fuller's management. Having said he is acting in order to help realize a more democratic state, Brutus adds a second motive, less noble but wonderfully human.

> And then society, aghast,
> Reeling against the statue, also will
> Be shocked to think I had a secret passion. . . .

This is turning his image to good account; but this expression of "won't they be surprised" is made humorous by the speaker's unintentionally exaggerated self-aggrandizement conveyed by "aghast," "reeling," and "shocked." The next line sustains and adds to the comic effect, "Though passion is, of course, not quite the word." The dramatic pose of the preceding line is seen as no more than that with the speaker worrying over the problem of precise wording. Given the occasion and circumstances we can hardly think other than that Brutus is miscast. But this movement is closed off by two lines of scenic description, "The dawn comes moonlike now between the trees/And silhouettes some rather muffled figues."

We are reminded that what is being planned is real enough by the arrival of the conspirators and that private fantasy and the niceties of diction will be swallowed up by events. The final half dozen lines constitute another unit of effect and similarly blend the fastidious, the self-depracatory, the comic-pathetic to set up and provide a touching context for the final assertion of courage,

> It is embarassing to find oneself
> Involved in this clumsy masquerade. There still
> Is time to send a servant with a message:
> "Brutus is not at home": time to postpone
> Relief and fear. Yet, plucking nervously
> The pregnant twigs, I stay. Good morning, comrades.

We may catch in the repetition of the word "time" an echo of Eliot's "The Love Song of J. Alfred Prufrock" with its loaded use of the word. What is particularly chilling as Brutus speaks of time is the sense that he is reflecting momentary impulse rather than defining a real possibility. As the lines move to their close we recognize that already events and not Brutus possess the moment. A fine touch is the word "relief" which emerges with something of a surprise, since flight and postponement logically imply a means of gaining relief. The seeming break in meaning naturally draws special attention to the word and underlines the deep concern of Brutus which sustains him in face of his obvious aversion and fear and earns him our empathy. The two adjectives "clumsy" and "pregnant" are of special interest because they pull in opposite directions and enact in miniature the semicomic mix of the whole passage. Within context, "clumsy" gives the whole enterprise an air of being both absurd and ill-conceived and does not augur well for its success. As well it suggests a heavy-handed crudeness. "Pregnant" counters "clumsy," connoting in one sense a fragile immaturity while registering a note of poignancy. Clearly it also relates itself to the plotting which will give birth to goodness knows what in a bath of blood. Thoughts of birth inevitably stir thoughts of death. The functioning of "good" is self-evident, and "morning" in this situation readily conveys mourning. Finally, the concluding word "comrades" anachronistically calls to mind the kind of political brutality which a younger Fuller eschewed.

The second of the dramatic poems, named for the protagonists of Beethoven's opera *Fidelio*, is the most enigmatic item in the collection. The speaker in "Florestan to Leonora" apparently has been a political prisoner under a tyranny. On the occasion of the poem, the prisoner, with "the oppressor" dead, is being given his freedom. Unexpectedly this fills him with distress, because now "values must shrivel to the size of those/Held by a class content with happiness"; and because he has become inured to incarceration—"Did you never conceive that it was possible/To like incarceration?"—he is terrified that his ability to meet the demands of Leonora's love have been eroded. Is the poem to be read literally? a statement, say, of how radicalism or dedication can function only in adversity, or, is the whole a metaphor for a more autobiographical predicament? This latter can be supported by cross references to two neighboring poems. "Florestan to Leonora" begins, "Our shadows fall beyond the empty cage." A possible clue to a special meaning for "cage" may be observed in a statement in "The Final Period," "Life goes on offering alarms/To be imprisoned in the cage/Of art." Conceivably, then, the poem is a fictive presentation of the poet about to withdraw from the intense, living, perhaps even violent mood of creativity and return to the banality of the everyday world. This possible reading is given further credence by "Jag and Hangover" which is a literal rendering of this transition. The second of its six stanzas is the most explicit for illustrative purposes,

> The muse's visitations
> Fatigue and inflame the sense,
> Are precisely as intense
> For McGonagalls as for Donnes:
> The word appears and stuns
> The power to see the true relationships.

"Florestan to Leonora" may even express some slight residual nostalgia, with the poet harkening back to the intense drama of the imprisoning war years viewed from the perspective of a "starved" welfare state existence. In any case, the poem demonstrates an ever-increasing tendency in Fuller to release himself into more adventuresome stances.

Providing an impressive and colorful conclusion to *Brutus's Orchard* are nineteen "Mythological Sonnets." Written with verve and a great sense of fun—one senses the poet's stimulation with a fresh order of images—they look back to various stages of past history from the perspective of the present, often contrasting the periods, though more frequently celebrating the enduring potency of the female. These poems may come from the same area of conception which produced "Translation" and "The Ides of March," but here the specific matter is chiefly Homeric and Ovidian: a landscape complete with unicorns and centaurs. Immediately preceding these sonnets is "To a Friend Leaving for Greece" which speaks of

> Greece, with its islands like discovered bones,
> Its names of our neuroses and its youth
> Made dark "with fabulous accounts and traditions."

What makes most of the sonnets possible is the poet's assumption of omniscience and the opportunity it provides for viewing two scenes simultaneously. Juxtapositioning is the working principle. The first sonnet is highly representative in both subject matter and procedure,

> Far out, the voyagers clove the lovat sea
> Which fizzled a little round its oily calms,
> Straw sun and bleached planks swinging, the
> Gunwale ribbed with a score of tawny arms.
> Nursing a bellyache, a rope-rubbed hand

> Or a vague passion for the cabin boy,
> Accustomed to the rarity of land
> And water's ennui, these found all their joy
> In seeing the hyphens of archipelagos
> Or a green snake of coast rise and fall back.
> And little they imagined that in those
> Inlets and groves, stretched out as on the rack
> Their girls were ground under the enormous thews
> Of visiting gods, watched by staid munching ewes.

This technique of the ironic overview is one bridge between Fuller's poetry and fiction, for a recurring fact of the novels is the interplay between an individual's circumscribed awareness of his situation and of the reader's awareness of manipulative outside forces. The drama of the novels involves the protagonist's gradual and generally painful journey to a position from which he himself shares the vision previously accorded the reader. Omniscience in the fiction serves suspense and dramatic situation; in the poetry it provides humor and wry comment. The overall point the sonnets have to make is the chastening one that we must not take present truth as any absolute. Sonnet "V," for example, tells how those who lived through the supposedly heroic experience of the Greco-Trojan War could hardly be expected to envision "the extent of time's appalling trick" which would save from the great scene "some kitchen pot."

A concern of several sonnets is the continuing validity of myths, which allow the covert in life to find expression. But more than anything else "Mythological Sonnets" celebrate the eternal female. Sonnet "XI" is a compact history of the altering styles of women down through history; but whatever conceptions have been in fashion all women, down to the contemporary shopgirl, have shared qualities with the fabulous goddesses. This is the sestet,

> Even the most sere and opulent
> Goddesses rise from the sordid life of man,
> Who catching, say, a girl in stockinged feet
> Arranging a shop-window sees the event
> Translated to a new and staggering span
> Of art, the previous pantheon obsolete.

Sonnet "XIV" says the power of the female is "never ruled but for an hour" and outlasts that of the male. The source of male potency comes at last to be a virtual irrelevancy,

> Towards the temple stride young girls whose dress
> Taut with the zephyr of their passage, shows
> The secret lack which men initially
> Despise, then eye with tragic covetousness,
> And lastly envy, conscious of the blows
> Time hammers on their superfluity.

To conclude this consideration of *Brutus's Orchard* with the image of the female—for instance, "Two tender virgins lying naked"—would be appropriate insofar as the libidinous is to be an ever increasing motif in subsequent volumes; but, in fact, the closing word of the volume is "guilt"—"violent dreams of Guilt"—and that, taking the work on the whole, is the most fitting final notation.

III   Collected Poems 1936-1961

The first six of the seven sections into which *Collected Poems 1936-1961* is divided correspond to Fuller's previously published volumes with a very few of the earlier poems omitted. The seventh section consists of then recent and hitherto unpublished work. This I now consider.

The narrative and fictive tendencies of *Brutus's Orchard* become as well the dominant feature of this work which consists chiefly of two extended sequences, "Faustian Sketches" and "Meredithian Sonnets."

The eleven parts making up "Faustian Sketches" share several thematic concerns with "Mythological Sonnets," though they are not cast in the sonnet form and, in fact, are all formally different. While employing an omniscient observer for the last two poems, the author yields up his "I" to several other first-person performers, most notably the aging lust-frustrated Faust. These are lively poems, mostly in darting short lines, mixtures of comedy and pathos. As with previous "historical" poems, Fuller enjoys blending aspects of earlier times—here, for example, alchemy—with the contemporaneous, that is, "condoms."

The comically ironic is at its purest in "Faust's Servant" and "The Princes." This latter item depicts an invisible Faust visiting "a weighty congress" of diplomats and politicians which culminates in farcical slapstick after Faust boxes ears and ignites Chinese firecrackers. The partial consequences are, "Thrombosis, rupture,/ Incontinence of urine, rife in the hall!" But even this exposure of the thinness of international niceties has its qualifying note of pathos. Left alone after all of the potentates and their lackies have headed off to prepare for war, Faust knows that even wars among the planets could not "wound him more than his unease of soul." Man's burden is himself.

The fun of "Faust's Servant" results from the old man's total misreading of his master whom he believes, because of his apparent devotion to books, to be the very opposite of himself, totally absorbed in "feminine anatomy." Several poems make clear Faust's parallel absorption. The celebration of this anatomy leads to several fine descriptive lines:

> I saw the tights, chalk-white, unwrinkled,
> Full of their fated shapes,
>
> ("Faust and the Dancers")

> It staggers me to find between her thighs
> The gold that struck me with such awe when first
> I saw it like a halo round her head
>
> ("Helen")

It leads as well to the heaviness of soul Faust bears. Age is one villain; in "Faust and the Dancers" he cries, "What soul would I destroy/ To be a boy again!" But the greater villain is "the core/ Of living" itself which he characterizes as "That bleeding accident." The cruel self-defeating paradoxes of life which paralyze Faust in "Faust Bathing" because of his "aptness for intenser pain" is most movingly portrayed in "Gretchen." Gretchen, the speaker, recalling her willing loss of virginity to Faust, tells how the completed act left them with love stillborn. Faust knows why: only because he had forfeited his soul could he come to her, and the resultant soulessness of their embrace doomed them.

In the longest of these poems, "Dreams in the City," Faust has assumed the mantel of a poet (and the persona, as well, of Fuller himself, since he is the inhabitant of a larger city and is a suburbanite with a garden!). Ultimately the poem is about the creative act and the magic inherent in it and may be seen as a development from the refrain of the preceding poem, "Magic": "And magic is to set me free." At the close the speaker is experiencing that moment depicted in several Fuller poems of being in transit from the intense involvement in creativity to the daily world. Suddenly he is surprised, hearing "a terrifying aria," and only gradually comes to the realization that he himself is its source: "Can I be that improbable/ Singer, this the unlikely song?" The drama of the poem resides in the dynamics of the protagonist's mind as it moves from thought to thought, registers a streetscape slowly filling "with golden light," then, gathering energy, soars into a vision of revelation. The earlier and major portion of the poem, operating on a routine plane of speculative observation, has seemed to deny the impossibility of the imaginative leap given both the depressing times and "indifference" of the speaker; but the creative imagination is shown to work in strange ways its wonders to disclose. Hence the conclusive, surprised response, the waking into normative self-consciousness. The view first propounded is that prosperous modern man, a dweller in cities, is a dreamer, since "The luxury of cities prompts/ Deluded dreams." The speaker recognizes that he shares this tendency—specifically, he dreams of writing "astounding words" and of being the great saving lover, for he fantasizes himself abducting "from her Duke/ The grave clever beauty, starved of love." These dreams are, of course, opiates and as such conducive to indifference about life. Thus it is natural to think that real changes can come only from "devout ascetics" who eschew the corrupting life of cities. But the poem becomes a demonstration of the falseness of this belief. Even the confined nature of the urban garden can stir the imagination to saving conceptions: the higher dream, the imaginative vision is enabled to break through the lesser dreams of fantasy. The title, "Dreams in the City," proves to have an initially unexpected double meaning.

The second multiple work is very much concerned with life in the city. This is the "superb sonnet sequence," "Meredithian Sonnets," twenty-one poems of sixteen lines.[3] The initial sonnet introduces the central theme of suffering and distinguishes between the suffering artist who can find "compensations that will cancel out/ The thing" and the ordinary man who lacks a consoling resource in creativity. The remaining sonnets follow a middle-aged nonartist through scenes from his life in the city, recording his experiences, his sufferings, and his thoughts, while bringing out his capacity for stoical acceptance. Details of the protagonist's past are vague and generalized, presumably in order to make him a representative individual. It seems he married and proved impotent, this latter a consequence, so he

believes, of childhood experiences which haunt him but which
he himself cannot fully grasp. The hints suggest he was
enmeshed in the feminine, both mother and sister, and so
idealized it as to make him incapable of violation. In any case, the
origins of his troubles are not as significant as the present sadness
of his life and his endless contact and fascination with the women
of the city. Nothing draws him more than that which causes most
pain. This figure somewhat resembles the outsider frequently
portrayed in the poetry of Philip Larkin. By comparison Fuller's
man is not so tough, self-puncturing, or self-justifying and is
therefore more shadowy and wistful. Sonnet "II" may be cited as
representative of the mood and imagery of the series:

> Great suns, the streetlamps in the pinhead rain;
> Surfaces gradually begin to shine;
> Brunettes are silvered; taxis pass in line
> On tyres that beat through moisture like a pain.
> Doubtless upon such evenings some at least
> Of those events that shaped his soul occurred:
> Against the streaming glass a whispered word
> Whitened and faded, and the shapeless beast
> Drank from the dripping gutters through the night.
> But all the child expressed and feared is long
> Forgotten: only what went wholly wrong
> Survives as this spectator of the flight
> Of lovers through the square of weeping busts
> To happiness, and the lighted towers
> Where mad designs are woven by the powers;
> Of normal weather, ordinary lusts.

The opening of "IV"—"The worker columns ebb acrosss the
bridges"—recalls a scene from "The burial of the Dead," and I
note this reference to the century's most famous city poem in
order to register the normality of "Meredithian Sonnets." They
forcefully capture the actual feel of many facets of life as
experienced by a sensitive urbanite. Additional quotation from
"IV" will make the point,

> The worker columns ebb across the bridges,
> Leaving the centre for the few ablaze.
> In bars, fox terriers watch their masters raise
> Glass to moustache; and rain streams from the ridges
> Of blackened balustrades and capes of girls.

> To death and rubbish theatres resound:
> Dummies in shops imperfectly expound
> The nude: throats raise the temperature of pearls.
> Luxury and moderate gaiety disguise
> The flights of coin, the absence of ideas.

This sonnet concludes with a finely incisive line, summing up from the viewpoint of one of the unblessed what it is "to live in mortal cities—/Haunted by trivial music, stomach tensed." If one is sympathetic to what Fuller is recording in this work then it is difficult not to feel these poems could hardly be improved upon and that Fuller is working at the top of one particular bent. The poet displays striking versatility in varying the treatment of his protagonist and "the small affairs that stab him to the heart."

Three of the remaining poems are among Fuller's finest. "Monologue in Autumn" is an evocative densely wrought miniature novel in eighty-four lines, a rare kind of poem in recent British poetry. The speaker is married to a wealthy woman who does not reciprocate the deep love he has for her. He is a man in a dilemma. Caught between his love and the intense dislike he holds for their way of life, the selfish existence of the privileged, he survives because "love has learned the trick of suffering/ Its object's relative indifference." Her attitude stems largely from impatience with his social concerns and guilt feelings. The mood of dying autumn on their estate is beautifully evoked; but most impressive is the skillful management of imagery. The full significance of the opening images of ruthlessness and violence linked to the elegantly artificial only gradually discloses itself,

> With yellow teeth the hunter tears and crunches
> Whole boughs of quince, then walks away,
> His hind legs on a mannequin's straight line.

A few lines later the wife appears and the protagonist helps her mount, her "body in its carapace/ Of steel and leather." Subsequently we realize the poet has given us, with great economy, a characterization of the tough, rapacious power which makes possible this mannequin world of wealth. Later, from within the stately home, a second and contrasting depiction of this world in its essential arrogant emptiness is offered,

In the drawing room
The fire sadly burns for no one: soon
Your guests will descend, taste tea on Sunday tongues,
Their lives and mine and yours go on with talk,
The disposition of chairs and lamps, the opened
Doors to the terrace, the order of good-nights.

The poem comes full circle with a reprise for horses and
destructiveness—"dead branches/ Threading the sockets of
those equine skulls/ Whose riders perished in the useless war"—
and thus quickly are the imperialistic pretensions of the
aristocracy and their necessary sacrifice in the name of
nationalism brought home. It is not difficult to extrapolate a
simple allegorical reading of "Monologue in Autumn." The
speaker, a representative Englishman, is in a love-hate relationship with his wife who symbolizes imperialistic-aristocratic
England.

"Versions of Love" also deals with the anguish of love and in a
very original manner. The speaker, reading a play, speculates
about a long-standing textual problem it has raised. Though no
author is named, and the textual problem is a fictious one, the
dramatist in question appears to be Shakespeare. At issue are
likelihood and desire. The line of text in question reads in "the
Bad Quarto," "My love for you has faded." This statement strikes
the speaker as so painful that he instinctively wants to believe
the emendation, on human if not on scholarly grounds, "My love
for you fast endured." The real strength of the poem comes in
the climactic reconstruction of the situation out of which the
aging dramatist may be thought to have actually written,

But this conjecture cannot quite destroy
The question of what the poet really wrote
In the glum middle reaches of his life:
Too sage, too bald, too fearful of fiasco
To hope beyond his wife,
Yet aching almost as promptly as a boy.

Having found the pose of a Roman intellectual congenial and
fruitful in "Translation" and "The Ides of March," Fuller turns to
it for a third time in "On the Mountain." The protagonist is here
older than his predecessors as well as less emotional, more
thoughtful, and, finally, more hopeful (befitting the mood of "a

final period" earlier announced in the closing portion of
Collected Poems). This really means the emphasis has shifted
from vituperative anger and dramatic involvement to a more
extended critique of the state of contemporary society. Once
more the poet employs his fun-enhancing strategy of the
anachronistic, so that such Roman references as "gladiatorial
games" are no more than the thinnest veil thrown over present
times. Some references retain the capacity to be both ancient
and modern simultaneously, "hill of villas" and "the borders of
the empire." But these really set up the operative statements of
disclosure: "The theatres are given up to leg shows"; "In poetry
the last trace of conviction/Has long since been extinguished";
"Atrocious taxes to 'defend' the frontiers;/ Fixing maximum
prices";

> The so-called educated classes share
> The superstitions and amusements of
> The vulgar, gawping at guts and moaning singers.

and the catalog—distressingly? delightfully?—goes on. Not
unsurprisingly the speaker finds some consolation and comfort in
literature:

> I find a little comfort in recalling
> That complaints of evil times are found in every
> Age which has left a literature behind:
>
> And that the lyric is always capable
> Of rejuvenation (as is the human heart).
> Even in times of general wretchedness.

These lines prompt me to recall the closing lines of the earlier
poem, "Obituary of R. Fuller": "Whether at this we weep or
laugh/ It makes a generous epitaph." The lines from "On the
Mountain" are so absolutely central to Fuller's sentiments that
they do indeed make a highly appropriate rounding off to this
survey of *Collected Poems*.

CHAPTER 4

Later Poetry

T HE poetry in Fuller's last four volumes, *Buff* (1965), *New Poems* (1968), *Tiny Tears* (1973), and *From the Joke Shop* (1975), continues the general tendencies of the previous work but does show new points of emphasis. As a whole the poetry is less dramatic than that of the middle period and contains a higher percentage of light verse. As one critic remarks, "A little late comedy is in keeping with the opus."[1] Most striking of the new tendencies is an interest in the irrational and "the entrance into the style of an order other than logic."[2] One may sense a form of compensation acting: as the experiences of daily existence narrow down, and the drier reaches of an actual final period endured, stimulation is found in thinking about the potential of the chaotic and irrational underpinnings of life now no longer viewed as threat so much as challenge to the fixed and life-draining patterns of living. The "wild" tendencies of the libido, though far from new in Fuller, are a fruitful preoccupation. His interest in the otherness of the phenomanal world is opened up as never before.

A considerable body of this work also justifies Fuller's being characterized as a garden or backyard poet. The realm of little domesticated nature is a frequent springboard for the ruminations of the familar persona of the withdrawn but thoughtful urbanite who now is retired and, because of poor health, repeatedly drawn to the questions of illness and death. As the epigraph to *Buff* hints at, a new law comes into play through much of this verse: any increase in the speaker's pain is balanced by an equivalent increase in his humor.

I   Buff

Buff contains some very effective light verse and begins to display Fuller's fascination with the irrational; but the most impressive work is found in two long sequences which appear to emerge from the same mood which produced much of the work in *Brutus's Orchard*. The twenty-five Shakespearean sonnets of "The Historian" are a counterpart to the earlier "Mythological Sonnets" and redeploy many of their concerns and characteristics. More original and truly a poetic tour de force is "To X," a twenty-one part narrative sequence in Fuller's dramatic vein. A useful way of approaching this particular poem is by way of considering the volume's epigraph. This, which is the source for the title, is from an old forfeits game: "'Methinks Buff smiles./ 'Buff neither laughs nor smiles.' " This is enigmatic and is, I think, meant to be in the interest of encouraging a complex response in the reader and in indicating a particular attitude on the part of the author. Buff probably embraces both the idea of fate, or the blows of fate as in blindman's buff, and the state of nakedness. Certainly "To X" is a fateful exposure. The Buff who neither laughs nor smiles may be the poet who wishes to indicate that his portrayal of the protagonist is in no sense an exercise in fun or satire.

What is immediately impressive about "To X" is its technical virtuosity, consisting as it does of twenty-one roundels, a punishing accomplishment, since the form consists of thirteen ten-syllable iambic lines with the first line repeated as the seventh and thirteenth lines, and the second line repeated as the eighth; the whole is restricted to two rhymes, a b b a a b a b and a b a a. That the resulting novel in miniature is sustained with remarkable inventiveness and with apparent ease is impressive. George Macbeth calls this Fuller's finest poem "and one of the best love poems of the century."[3] Another critic, Ian Hamilton, while admiring the work qualifies his praise, believing the form leads to "somewhat pedantic engineering."[4] One can understand the origins of Hamilton's complaint, but I think he underestimates the extent to which the restrictive form, the engineering, with its deliberate formal strains and stresses, helps create the meaning.

The poem is narrated retrospectively by a middle-aged bachelor poet of some fame. His apparent motive in relating this experience of unfulfilled love is presumably self-justification. When the narrative has unfolded sufficiently we begin to sense the gap between the protagonist's insight into what has happened and the truth which is tied up with his psychology. The success of the poem, then, stems from the relationship between the complex inner state of the speaker and the strained intricacy of the stanzas.

The story line is simple enough. To the seaside resort where the bachelor poet is holidaying comes the young woman, accompanied by her husband, with whom he conducts an outwardly modest unconsummated affair. Part "II" records her arrival and the protagonist's first glimpse of her:

> The car arrived that brought you to the place:
> As you got out I saw your very groin.
> Thus goddesses, nude upon a distant quoin
> Reveal their chaste religion to the race.
>
> The aged, usual guests who sit or pace,
> By chance I casually wandered out to join:
> The car arrived that brought you to the place;
> As you got out I saw your very groin.
> Later it seemed impossible to trace,
> As you politely spooned your macedoine,
> That I had known the dark skin near the loin;
> Already in another time and space
> The car arrived that brought you to the place.

The actual development of the relationship, though not without narrative interest, is secondary to the psychological drama which the poet undergoes both at the time and subsequent to their farewell. Since it is being written after the fact, "From the great distance of the end of caring" ("XXI"), the poem abounds in self-immolating irony. Here is an instance from "VI":

> To find oneself still capable of pain
> Was direly reassuring, being old;
> As though an organ long thought spent had told
> Of its strong presence through the chemist's stain.

The intricate, even artificial nature of the stanzas operates in one direction to support the throw-away attitude, the at times almost comical recapitulation. The speaker, in part, is instinctively soliciting our support for his position by suggesting that he is subjecting his story to vigorous open-eyed scrutiny. But more importantly, the elegant formalism makes possible and controls a touching pathos. The pain is built unobtrusively by tiny

strokes. First, there is an inevitable discovery to be made about
his beautiful goddess,

> But sitting idly in the mirrored hall
> Which showed an image awkward, almost base,
> And suddenly I saw that, after all,
> It was imperfect your thought perfect face.

And gradually it comes back to him that consummation is not the
central fact of such an engagement, "Shaken by longing, how can
one conceive/That longing is the essence of it all?" Perhaps the
most chastening rediscovery is that "the gift" of making "dearth
richness" is "in disrepair" ("XV"). Further chastening rediscov-
eries accumulate, but the feeling is always distanced by the form.
The artifice contributes to the complex total effect in at least
two ways. First, it helps convey the true nature of the protagonist
who in his fastidiousness and self-consciousness cannot let
himself go, who would inherently prefer form to substance,

> I knew how mean and ludicrous the thing,
> Not only in itself but on the age,
> Daily I opened a disturbing page
> And cringed to think that very day must bring
>
> Our confrontation. That I could not wring
> Good from the storms that private man engage,
> I knew how mean and ludicrous. The thing
> Not only in itself but on the age....

This compassionately implies the reason individuals have
difficulty in fully comprehending intense personal situations. "To
X" is a remarkable presentation of the workings of memory and
rationalization and a prime demonstration of Fuller's artistic
resourcefulness.

Relationships between the sexes, from a masculine viewpoint,
are the subject of several poems, chiefly in a light mood. The
males are anything but robust lovers and obviously incapable of
fulfilling the demands of their feminine counterparts. "A Wife's
Unease" examines the change which has taken place in the needs
of the poet protagonist's wife. When a "slim brown-haired girl"
she had picked the poet "Because she felt him nobly different."
Since she was prepared to accept his self-regarding ego as the

price of distinction she in effect "pressed her lips against the mask of art." But now, years later, having "somewhat run to seed," her desires have altered: "Now it was rich/Vulgarity and thoughtlessness she craved."

Something of a variation generates "The Truth About Pygmalion" with its refrain "Do not image I was glad she breathed." Why? Because, as another recurring line informs us, "Suddenly appetite and longing seethed." A related poem is "Orpheus Beheaded" which may be seen as one answer to "Sailing to Byzantium" since it rejects a commitment to the intellectual life as represented by Orpheus's head. Orpheus finds himself, following his division, still capable of song; but it is not long before he makes a surprising discovery:

> I never thought to mourn my sordid tripes,
> But, ending in a bunch of bleeding pipes,
> I found the mind nostalgic for the gripes.

"Fifteen Foolish Encounters" consists of fifteen couplets, related by their delightful recording of the female, such as, "Her going left behind her in the room/A girl-shaped cloud of unalloyed perfume." These poems testify to the unceasing fascination women hold for men and to the goodwill they deserve whatever the vagaries of individual members of the species, "As her departure left him in the hell/ Of loss, he wished her, and all the species, well."

The second of *Buff's* long sequences consists of twenty-five quasi-Shakespearean sonnets under a title which identifies their persona, "The Historian." He is an aged scholar who ponders in his study under the lessons of history and the strange conjunctions it brings to pass. Fuller is clearly paying a return visit to approximately the same territory occupied by the "Mythological Sonnets" of *Brutus's Orchard*. The presence of the historian, however, is felt much more than that of the earlier unidentified commentator. In the case of both sequences the real effect is in the movement from poem to poem, in the exploratory fertility of the poet's mind, and is therefore cumulative.

As might be anticipated, most of the sonnets play with contrasts and ironical paradoxes which the speaker produces by juxtaposing contemporary aspects of society with their earlier counterparts: the literal eunuchs of old are introduced to set off

their figurative modern brethern, the males who almost
unawares are gradually gelded ("VI"); as we puzzle over aspects
of older civilizations, so we can image future generations
bewildered by modern objects ("X"); strange to say, the
ancients, while crueller and cruder in many ways, were also more
cultured ("XII"); a student of history can repeatedly observe
how men are capable of debating the nature of freedom
endlessly—until their thoughts are drawn to their own approaching deaths("XIV"); the great figures who seek to gain general
approval through deceit, the "Haters of truth," are destined to
become "its stuff at last" ("XV"); experience teaches one to
grasp that the reason youthful Paris chose Venus was because
Juno and Minerva were "too womanly" for him ("XX"); and it is
possible to trace out the relationship between the altering shape
of women and the evolution of mechanical engineering
("XVIII").

The impact of barbarians and vandals upon civilization comes
in for repeated consideration and the historian's culminating
insight is that "Should the barbarians not be at hand/A disolute
culture will destroy itself" ("VIII"). The revelation in "IX" is that
the greater in both history and the human body forever falls to
the lesser: "History turns . . . from democracy to lethal whims . . .
in violent hippodromes" while the body's "citadels/Fall to
proliferating barbarous cells."

If a particular sonnet links "The Historian" with the central
material of *Buff* it is "IV" which distills the special flavor of the
collection as the historian turns his attention to his students,

> Even more brilliant pupils will possess
> Illusions neither reason nor disdain
> Eradicate. Astonishing to find
> The young full lips, set off by hair and dress
> In a bizarre contemporary strain,
> Voicing opinions fatuous or blind.
> Though even those tender mouths themselves, I guess,
> Are put to uses I would think quite vain—
> Imprinting merely their own callow kind.
> That fear and credulity led to excess
> In judging the Vandals' numbers, I explain
> Once more. It does not need that to remind
> My cultured heart of cracks made by decay
> Through which the stunning and uncaring stray.

This sonnet and several others strike a subjective note which permit us to glimpse the man beneath the historian. For students of Fuller these may be the most attractive of the poems. It is the sense of the human response, the recurring motif of subdued sadness, which gives the sequence texture and prevents it becoming simply a series of ironical insights. In one of the most forceful sonnets, "XVI," the speaker notes his own inability, even with the knowledge he commands, to profit more from the lessons of history:

> Impoverished and in lonely
> Opposition, even at the stadium I—
> Unlike the rearing mass—admire the skills
> Impartially. In fact, my hope is only
> That blood will not be spilt and that each side
> Will with defeat be somehow satisfied.

Self-effacing in any case, he accepts his own insignificance, "Youth that brings down or hoists the crown looks past/My work and face with equal indifference" ("XV"). He is at odds with his milieu where, for instance, "cranes pile cell on cell/To some great lucrative aesthetic blunder" ("XVI"). All this casting of a jaundiced eye across a catalog of folly and absurdity may be viewed as preparatory for the final poem. In spite of his passive alienation the historian is not without hope and can envision because of his belief in the innate goodness of the general masses a world with wars and prejudice ended and men happy at last "with their soilskinned globe."

Another historical moment is depicted in "Brahms Peruses the Score of Siegfried" which carries the informing subtitle, "The photograph by von Eichholz." This is one more representative moment of change or, more precisely, moment of unrecognized change, for it memorializes man's inability to register the destructive presence of counterforces. The first five stanzas calmly offer a verbal counterpart of the photograph. Then, in the concluding stanza, the poet shifts the mood sharply, crying,

> But how can he not be falling back aghast
> At the chromatic spectrum of decay,
> Starting to destroy already
> His classical universe.

The verse form will be seen to provide a formal counterpart to the issue at hand.

"Brahms Peruses the Score of Siegfried" might be said to offer a choice, Brahms or Wagner, that is, a choice between the classical or rational and decadent romanticism, the new barbarism, or the irrational. What engages Fuller in other poems, those displaying the adventuresomeness of the collection, is the clashing or admixture of separate yet related spheres, the rational or explicable up against the mysteriously irrational. This is treated overtly in "Homage to Dr. Arnold Gesell and to My Grand-Daughter Sophie." Gessell comes in for admiration because he is interested in the origins of baby talk and the relationship between early and subsequent verbal characteristics. This is an area revelatory of subjective psychological struggles, "Since ordered language is most loath to admit/The excited dreamsoaked gibberish of its start." What interests is the strata underlying the articulate where always exists "A struggle with the uncommunicable,/A chanter of enchantment."

The more covert treatments of this concern enact the uneasy concourse between the daytime areas of being and those of the nighttime, and wonder how they relate and how they actually intrude upon one another. In his willingness to allow the inexplicable to remain, Fuller realizes a new kind of poem for himself. "Logic of Dreams" has the freshly awakened mind recalling the dreams of the night and trying to submit their strangeness to the process of rationalization, but "It is hard to imagine how dreams contrive/To deposit one nude before mad girl-faced apes." Dreams, the speaker believes, haunt because more intense than actual experience and purer in emotional origin. He says, "How much more convincing, the time of dreams" and suspects the quality of life relates to the state of the subconscious. "Impoverished wakening to unrecalled dreams:/Start of a day empty of dreaming's source."

The protagonist and his situation in "Brother Serene" truly suggests Fuller has entered into fresh imaginative territory. Serene is a monastic who has withdrawn from the world for reasons he cannot quite grasp: "What brought me here? The quest for a father?" It seems more likely he feared the world, or both feared and craved authority. Whatever his impetus Serene is not alone, for his order is bulging with novices. They may have entered in pursuit of simplicity and in an attempt to escape confusion "of every irrelevant kind"; but the quirk in the situation is that the ironically named Serene cannot respect that which he craves.

Similar fateful inexplicables are recorded in "Sister Anne" and "The King and the Goose-Girl." In the latter the girl is capable of gazing through the monarch to the country shepherd; the king who can respond to her beauty lets "the epoch live in dread." The unidentified speaker can only shake his head at the "Prodigal curiosities" of his world "that will arrange/A future still more diverse and strange." "Sister Anne" is sinister in depicting the young bride eager "To gain the dreamed-of bower" while unaware of what her brother can forsee, "The gore, the constricted room." These poems, along with "By the Lake" and "Love and Murder" help make *Buff* a well-rounded collection; they are disturbing and allusive and may be said to pick up rocks in order to peer beneath them. They are certainly another reason why Buff neither laughs nor cries.

The various personae of *Buff* all emerge in some sense beleaguered. They are either disappointed in their own capacities as lovers or robust livers, or in the perverse nature of life and their own interior beings. A line in "Bagatelles" reads, "Useless to the lover, the breasts of his beloved" and one could say, "There, that is the poet in a nutshell—accentuating the negative and, in fact, going out of his way to do so." But to say this is too easy and too inadequate. There is no denying that a "weary scepticism" informs much of this work, but a full response recognizes the reverse side of the coin as well. Ian Hamilton properly sees within this work "a degree of wisdom and honest self-analysis that is rare and useful in contemporary poetry."[5] It is not, finally, that Fuller is overly conscious of the disasters and disturbances both within and without that circumscribe the individual quest for a meaningful life, but that he never loses his self-possession and never despairs of finding compensatory factors. The concluding lines from "Favouring the Creatures" provide a revelatory summing up:

> Incredible to have seen
> In fifty years' destruction
> Afternoons of timid paws
> And comical conversations.

II New Poems

Of Fuller's final four volumes *New Poems* is both the most original and the strongest. The originality stems from an engagement with the metaphysical. Having in recent volumes shown a fondness for glancing backward in time with an ironically tilted historical perspective, Fuller now becomes fascinated with the spiritual world which can be thought to interface with the physical world of man, the realm of an alternate "order"— the word recurs from poem to poem—made up of natural divinities. The outlook bears some resemblance to that assumed to be held by the early Greeks toward their milieu.

In "The Visitors" the poet expresses surprise at his unexpected consciousness of adjacent dimensions:

> No one could be more suspicious than I of
> The sudden appearance of divinities
> In middle-age verse, but how else to describe
> The double nature of nature in epochs
> Of creative happiness?

Predictably these poems show the author less interested in the spiritual realm per se, than in exploiting it as a fresh avenue to the order of mankind; perhaps it is more accurate to view it as the fresh means of energizing his poetry it proves to be. Noting, in "Orders," that he has always felt himself separate from the masses, his desire "Always so different from the general will!" the speaker decides he will ally himself with the nonhuman: "Very well:/Assign the business of being a poet/To an order of things entirely divine"; but this is no more than a passing impulse. Once having made, as it were, a declaration of independence, the poet accepts his incapacity for turning his back on humanity: his true position is "(in Kafka's terms)/Of a wound that precisely fits the arrow."

Like *Buff, New Poems* offer the directive of an epigraph, this time from Hölderlin,

> A mystery are those of pure origin,
> Even song may hardly unveil it.
> For as you began, so you will remain.

Hölderlin's skepticism about the limitations of language to express complex human experience obviously stimulated Fuller to think about dimensions which may exist beyond the world of normal consciousness. But the epigraph suggests that penetration of the veil is possible, if only momentarily. Typically, Fuller's gods and goddesses prove both compassionate and needful of their human counterparts. What, the poet asks, "if outselves became divine and fell/On the pitiful but attractive human. . . . Would we not afterwards try to get back those/Beautiful offspring, so mortal, so fated?" ("Orders"). So we can see that through the divinities he does join a different order, but only to discover they share his feelings for other men. In "Those of Pure Origin," the spirits of nature address man (and indicate as well that they too have read their Hölderlin!), and admit an interdependence with the mortal:

> The mad poet called us, untranslatably:
>
> "Those of pure origin"—left you to divine
> Whether we rise from phenomena or,
> Perhaps more likely, also require your presence,
> As the cathedral the plague, pity the war.

These pure voices provide advice for men, and as befits an order outside the physical, it is either illogical or suprarational: "Prefer the less likely explanation" and do not adjudge the movement of the stars as heavenly revolutions "But a lucky change of erotic fortune." They hold out hope as well: "so often you've been wrong why shouldn't/You be wrong about the extinction of man?" The student of Fuller is bound to smile to himself in recognizing that either the poet is putting words in the mouths of divinities or else he has been in touch with them for many years. Not that this observation in any way invalidates the quality of these lyrics.

The stimulating consciousness of the forces enclosing and periodically entering into substance—perhaps as "the restless empire of nature"—is treated in several additional works. In "Creeper" the "Probing filament" that has worked its way in through a window edge is asked, "what do you seek/In our affairs?" and the significance of its intrusion pondered. In "Disasters" the poet, detailing "a whole/Hierarchy of unease," comes to an understanding about man's involvement with the spiritual, "One sees how legends came to be invented"; but addressing a "Symbolist Creator," he wonders if it would have been better if less had been left "to chance and speculation?" Another question proves to be the answer, for "How else"

> Except through flight along the margin of the
> Permanent, heaving thing could its nature have
> So imprinted itself in our sternum pulse
> And arches of our insteps?

But this is by no means a final position and proves merely part of an ongoing argument, for it is challenged by a further question in "In Lambeth Palace Road": "what has earth/To do with the purposelessness of divinities?" This ongoing dialectic is one reason why the text of *New Poems* crackles with verbal force.

"In Lambeth Palace Road," highly autobiographical and the centerpiece of the collection, offers an explicit explanation for the poet's obvious stimulation,

> Since at the moment
> The Springs of verse are flowing after a long
> Spell of being bunged up.

The poem is a deeply personal statement of affirmation and rededication. Registering a deep sense of affinity with the multifarious daily world, the poet joyfully confirms the worth of the quotidian. In a pensive mood, the speaker is seated in a tea shop adjacent to St. Thomas's Hospital near Waterloo waiting for the effects of radioactive treatment to wear off. He has before him two newspapers and *The Freud Journal of Lou Andreas-Salome*; he observes the waitress checking her lipstick and sees as well the desolate new concrete of developers' London. This is virtually the quintessential Fullerian situation, and the reader settles in anticipating the flow of the protagonist's thoughts.

From the start the poem is filled with contrasts and distinctions: the pigeon flying and the pigeon on the roadway "smeared as on a slide"; the ugliness of the surrounding urban buildings near the area "where Wordsworth found the earth most fair"; *The Times* and the *Evening Standard*. The poet draws sharp distinctions between men and women, the bourgeois and the cultural elite, even the bridge and the river—"such strange companions"—and, finally, the spiritual and the tangible. All of this is part of the strategy for a poem which rejects concern for "divinities":

> Is the universal order beneath the poet's
> Contempt, then? His sorrow for humanity,
> And its complex and pitiful body, too deep
> To be comprised in the dust and unneighbourly constellations?
> One must think so, submitting to the mercy of hospitals
> Agonized over disaster to birds, and drinking
> The real but small comfort of the Indian herb.

Elsewhere further facets of the conflict between compassion for the human condition and distress over human conduct are viewed. "Afternoons" worries over the general fate of women—"Poor Gorgons—/Doomed to decapitation in the very/Instant of parturition"—who must inhabit cityscapes "Snowing with fragments of brain, the pavement stained;/Debris of an exploded urban dream." Himself balanced between deep concern and sensuous appreciation, the speaker dryly addresses himself, "Come in/From your gazing at stockings long as prunus boughs."

The sharpest note of self-reproach occurs in "Reading *The Bostonians* in Algeciras Bay" when his political idealism of the thirties returns to haunt the poet in this setting. Sitting "deluxe" in "The realms of a tyrant of our youth" he knows "all is still to struggle for." He cries, "What a mess, societies of men!" acknowledging that "even Henry/Found history grave at last". An interesting aspect of this poem is the incorporation of a passage from *The Bostonians* as nine-syllable syllabic verse.

Self-deprecation in a lighter mood is the activity of several delightful works. "Chinoiserie" is a return to the old issue of life divided between business and art,

> It's a toss up whether I turn first
> To the literary or the financial page,
> And I find it just as painful to read
> Of a bonus issue of shares I failed to buy
> As of the success of a rival writer.

"Romance" ends with a list of items desirable in a more ideal world, one where

> . . . the wars are waged on a lower epicycle
> By armour diminutive as stag-beetles;
> And poets forbidden to sing of their diseases
> Or amatory botherations;
> And only with end-stopped irony.

Responding in "Road Safety" to a bumper sticker, "'watch my behind not hers'" the poet thinks he is doomed to crash from this very cause because of "inexhaustible/Generations achieving the age of eye-/Catching nubility." More substantial is "Departures," addressed to the poet's muse depicted as a mistress of long-standing. Fuller's myth of his being a modest poet from whom the muse aches "to depart" is given its due:

> Unworthy to receive your embrace,
> I'm always resolving to do much
> Better in future, an eternal
> Unsatisfactory boy; somehow
> Believing that I will, too.

The poem shifts from the poet's own relationship with this "sweetest girl" to a recognition of her involvement with an ambiguous world, for "dogged life itself must tempt you/To descend, or whirl to remotest/Quasars in flurries of apes."

The realm of art and the artist is the subject of four poems. In "The Painter" and "The Symphonist" the artists speak for themselves. The painter confronts the problem of subject matter; he rejects the depiction of any form of idealism and accepts that the public does not want paintings displaying unattractive aspects of life. And since, he states, "you can't/Have art be about nothing," the artist gets down to "the bowlishness of zinc bowls" (which is to subscribe to Gerard Manly Hopkins' sense of "inscape"). The symphonist is an old composer looking back over his career, rather confused now about the identity of his "just too many symphonies," recalling moments of intense delight and inspiration as well as "Seventeen years of complete silence," giving some insight into his working procedures— "quite outrageous conjunctions"—and concluding with an expression of self-awe, "To devote a whole life to wordless/Communication." "The Art of the Apple" celebrates the rich allusiveness of the apple. Considering the varied treatment of the fruit by painters over the centuries, the poet asks, "Confusing conspectus of periods and/Schools, how can we make up our minds about you?" "Astapove, 1910" envisions Tolstoy in his last minutes, offers a conspectus of his final unorthodox views, and comments upon them. Most interesting in the artistic context is the poet's own implied view about the origins of poetry. To Tolstoy's belief that "All true poetry is always/Outside" the sexual life, he replies, "One sees what he meant, though/ Reluctantly disagreeing."

New Poems concludes with "Last Sheet" which finds the poet making song out of his supposed limitations. Aging and with his "maladjusted gland" he muses, "A pity to have got so far along the road/And then never arrived." The concluding confession of artistic limitation, certainly a fruitful aspect of Fuller's personal myth, is stated with such seeming simplicity in this instance that it is difficult to register it as other than deeply held personal conviction. Though few writers choose to formalize their feelings in this regard, common experience suggests the universality of the gap between the artists' conceptions and their executions conveyed by these lines,

> This will have to stand, as usual,
> For the prodigies I was about to tell you of,
> For the connections I never quite saw, the melodies
> Played gently while the beauteous statue reconciled
> The jarred generations, and Sicily and Bohemia.

Fuller's poetry has never depended to any extent on literary allusion for effect; but this instance shows his touch in selecting and employing it tellingly.

III   Tiny Tears

Tiny Tears does not break new ground or hold any special surprises but continues to demonstrate Fuller's remarkable capacity for extending his observations and playing variations upon his by now well defined complex of interests. The recurring persona is of the poet as a withdrawn thoughtful man doubtful of both his adequacies as a writer and his effectiveness as a citizen. But what we can appreciate is the continuing vitality of the mind, if anything more sharply observant of its surroundings than ever, its honesty and fairness, and wise good-humor. The trick in reading Fuller is to see the truth of the pose while accepting it as a useful and intended to be understood convention. One biographical fact which enters into this work is the ill health of Fuller in these years. When such concerns as illness and aging are dealt with we have additional reason for believing Fuller is a poet who in the main is likely to appeal to an older reader.

This reference to a hypothetical representative reader is appropriate since the volume's opening poem is "To an Unknown Reader." It aims at achieving a conspiratorial rapport between the poet and his reader, implying they constitute a kind of secret society sharing possibly in a type of private vice, "Yet you read on, having kept, like a junkie,/The text for solitude." The poet suspects the reader is probably a frustrated poet—"a private bathroom vocalist"—and accordingly envious of the poet's own modest success. The poet, who cannot be other than what he is, urges the reader to consider that he may actually be better off as he is and asks if "dreams" are not

> better than syllable-counting,
> Than a whole lifetime's remorseful exposure
> Of a talent falling short of its vision?

But this question of vocation or role playing is simply preliminary to the real issue: the true function and value of poetry, what really prompts the poet to write and the reader to read. The essence of the matter is hope,

> And it's just
> That continuing expectation of words,
> Of opening portals, to promise more than they
> Really signify to which man's hope adheres.
>
> Alternatives to dead-ends of history
> Are what's conspiratorially offered. . . .

The rationale for beginning *Tiny Tears* with this poem is evident since the book sustains the ongoing process of renovation through creative attention.

The remaining poems in part "I" form three natural groupings. The first consists of garden poems, a consequence of the poet's ceaseless fascination with his domestic naturescape, his own grain wherein is found the universal. Both "Robins and Woodlice" and "Doves in a Tree" prompt what the speaker terms "half-baked thoughts of the Great/Chain of Being." The former work, explaining why he places a higher valuation on robins than woodlice, ponders his own place in the scale of matter. He concludes with the wry hope the powers above will display a similar kind of perspective and treat him with "meagre mercy." "Doves in a Tree" contrasts the love of birds, humans, and angels not to the detriment of the human since angels might very well "find our touch/Of palms an enviable thing."

"The Lawn, Spring and Summer" also leads to a confirmatory insight into the realm of men as opposed to the natural world. Discovering a baby bird's body on the grass the speaker is initially predisposed to see nature as "heroic." He feels immediate admiration for the mother bird's ability, "I salute your ruthless clearing of the decks"; yet further reflection leads him to qualify his response. After all, mankind really is the more heroic in generating and sustaining life in the face of inevitable "thwarted happiness."

Several of the shorter garden lyrics exist chiefly as sensuous imagery. One advantage of being a poet of fairly low imagistic wattage is that the striking lines arrive with special force. The tree in "Apple Tree" whose blossoms fall "flake on flake" is personified as an aging man,

> Limbs hugely knuckled, crooked, lines,
> What ecstasy for you to find
> The fair skin brush your dark rind.

In "Feathers," "threatening thunder blackens the loosened rose," And "One September" depicts "leaves inked on the west."

A second grouping consists of more subjective poems in which the speaker turns his attention to either his art or his health. Though the protagonist of "In the Radioactive Isotope Department" provides a comic depiction of himself undergoing a series of medical tests during which he seeks to appear calm and self-possessed—conducting himself with "false sangfroid." The results of the testing prove negative, so the experience has an immediately happy ending: "Only the covert gland has sinned." Yet the underlying sense of nervousness and fear remain, for the logic of the situation is confronted in the final stanza. Thoughts of a possible future reenactment are impossible to disperse,

> Is this the simple meaning—all
> Rehearsal for the moment when
> One buttons up one's shirt again
> And hears the sentence truly fall;
> While the fantastic myth of health
> That other organisms keep
> Goes on proliferating deep
> Philosophy, verse, love and wealth?

"Diary Entries", a series of ten four-liners, revisit various of the speaker's medical experiences, and reveal his ongoing concern for his health. In the midst he dryly comments, "A good thing also to stop writing verses/About one's ailment and daydreams of romance." The fact of aging and the role of imagination combine in a characteristic domestic milieu in "Late Period" and are realized through the image of a cat:

> After a few laps my old cat walks away
> From the saucer with an irritable jerk of tail:
> Five minutes later is back to try the stuff
> Again. And well I know the mood myself.

The speaker meanwhile has turned to another form of saucer, the record player, and listens to Brahms while wondering how long he will remain settled. Yet as nothing can replace food in the physical realm so now there are no alternatives to art in the spiritual,

> Yet what else but art
> Could I hope now might echo and assuage
> The tenderness and sadness of keeping house?

The imagined dreams of the sleeping cat and the master's flights on the wings of music are skillfully merged at the close. The cat "only hears its dreams. The claws retracted,/Murderous tonalities but softly clash."

Dreaming and aging likewise combine in the lengthy "The Final Period." The final war of his dreams—cast in the "anachronistic image" of World War II—is analogous to his physical state, "And so my tertiary period/Begins." The poem captures an intense period of worry. Everything appears negative, "Irregular metabolism turns/Even the era's joys to morbid waste." And one's role as artist shrinks to insignificance,

"Almost best/To have been the author of 'This stone was laid/By so-and-so on August 3rd.'" While we admire those who put on a brave face over serious illness we are conscious of the terror with which the lonely dying being must contend; this duality is what "The Final Period" conveys in an effectively dignified and subdued manner:

> Though always sleeping
> With it, one's never reconciled to death.
> And now to come so late in life to death
> By fire, death of the world, death of my art!
> I feel the pain of everything assaulted,
> Even boughs licked in rubbish-heaps of Autumn:
> Their boiling sap's my own.

If one survives to embrace again days of reasonable health, then one handles life with new appreciation. The final poem in this grouping, "Magnolia," expresses this. The title refers most immediately to the color of paint with which the poet's study has been redone. The refurbishing is emblematic of a new beginning and the poet says, "surely a fresh creative period/Opens." He is well aware "One can hardly go on with that depressing work" which has been occupying him and which at best can only be termed "stoical." Naturally enough the question is, what direction, what "Increasing of range is reasonably in prospect?" He feels naturally drawn to the "cyclical forces" of nature as an appropriate replacement for "the constant staleness of human blood."

A final group of three poems show Fuller at his most relaxed and fanciful. The works are linked by having some connection with Oxford where Fuller was then serving his five-year term as professor of poetry and where his son, the poet John Fuller, is a professor of English and the father of three daughters. "Mothy Invocation," in couplets, issues several directives to the insect beyond "the dark-backed window pane." These instructions begin as personal or familial—the moth is to fly westward to Oxford to "brush the foreheads fine" of his granddaughters and to touch his son "So verse of his may also run"—but then broaden out to encompass his wishes for the British Isles,

> Look, strange but not too alien face
> In all the dwellings of our race;

> Teach social order to be pure
> And personal failures to endure.

"To My Grand-Daughters," one of the most delightful of all Fuller poems, envisions the future when the three young girls will be three beauties of Oxford, "triple Zuleikas," "Enticing several years of/Freshmen," when their suitors will be "Caught in the hall by the expert on Auden," and at last when they marry ("The lucky but unworthy") and "(some will say)/Your hell's ministry resign."[6] Finally, "Edmond Halley" is a thumbnail history and character sketch of the onetime Oxford scientist. Playfully counterpoised are the "triumph of reason" which enabled Halley to foretell by fifty-five years the comet which subsequently bore his name, and the strange destiny which brought Fuller to Oxford. In old age Halley could eat only fish and pudding, and Fuller notes that he has arrived at Oxford "not far now from/the fish and pudding stage."

The activity of part "II" has been stimulated chiefly by current events or public occasions. "Confrontation off Korea, 1958" expresses the writer's attitude to international foolishness by presenting it in a series of comically concise and colloquial four line stanzas. It begins,

> Return our boat that you've
> Pinched from our serious play
> Or with another toy
> We'll roast you alive.

The poet's personal involvement with the crisis of the times produces the most typical verse,

> I pray that any nuclear war
> Will be deferred till after the
> Diminutive requirements for
> My coming book of poesy.

Poets are the subject of several poems. W. H. Auden's sixtieth birthday is marked by "To a Writer on His Birthday." With considerable adroitness Fuller manages within relatively few lines to evoke a sense of Auden's career and art and to record his personal debt to him. Fuller is forthright in complaining that the later Auden "burrowed too far into the lexicons" and in expressing regret at the elder poet's absence from England. He admits his criticisms are made with considerable apprehension, for "One can't ever lose the fear of being biffed by a stronger arm."

Three other poems on notable men mark the occasions of their passing. "In Memory of Randall Swingler and Alan Rawsthorne" and "Four Poems in Memory of Max Born" tend to the rhetorical but "At T. S. Eliot's Memorial Service" is a forceful rendering of mood and the speaker's attendant feelings at the Westminster Abbey observance. The long nine-beat line lends great weight and solemnity to the lyrical description: "Rectangles of iron-tubing for the Pensile lamps draw down the eye/To the choir-stalls' vandyke timber and their submarine upholstery." The poem achieves its fine climax by adroitly raising echoes of *The Waste Land*. The poet is departing from the service,

Tributory bowler on its not entirely unaccustomed head,
Leaving through the great West Door, bells muffled for the now-accepted dead,
All is changed until I see that it's Victoria Street and not the Square
Lies before me purgatory-crowded, hideous in the sharpening air—

Half expecting one to hail me, marks of mould upon him, grave of tone:
"Wounded still the Ruler, waterless the land, omnipotent the bone."

The poem's central point, the poet's particular reason for valuing Eliot, is indirectly stated, although the epigraph, from Jessie L. Weston's *From Ritual to Romance,* functions as a directive: "A man comes on stage ... and ... chants the Great Mysteries, not knowing what he says." Eliot made the mystery in which life is shrouded real and deeply felt. In this he was unlike the craftsmen who have created the artifacts in the Abbey and who "Celebrate the sad illusion that the mortal nerves and brain make sense." This contrast between ways of comprehending the earthly condition is subtly reinforced by the movement of the stanzas between the precisely seen—the "iron-tubing" description, for example, already cited—and the evocative unpenetrable—the "submarine upholstery." The poem implies as well that Eliot has now possessed his true element fully in entering "the unseen."

Another poet is directly involved in a witty sonnet. Fuller produces what Shakespeare apparently did not, "Sonnet 155."

The epigraph, "Two loves I have of comfort and despaire," is really a setup for the "confession" which follows. At issue is the contrast which exists between the love and lust of the speaker's art—where "No doubt one laid it on a thought too thick"—and his actual making out with the woman involved who unknowingly calls his bluff. She troubles about neither the look in his eyes nor the "sheaf of sonnets" but is all "brawling" business. Though he ends with an expression of pain it is not the one in a part "unsung" by him.

If the poet of part "I" of *Tiny Tears* is essentially that of the quiet private life, and of part "II" that of the public recorder, then in "III" he is chiefly that of the complex and allusive interior self.

The first seven poems, grouped under the general title "From an Old File," take the poet back into the memory banks of his wartime and postwar experiences.[7] "First Winter of War" and "Embarkation in Wartime" are mood poems and reinvoke the old sensations of fear and tightness of the stomach. "Diary Entry in the Fifties" depicts the writer's typical day as mundane, and belies the intense subjective theater of dreams, desires, fears, and myths he experiences and which are recorded in "Psychoanalyst to Poet," "The Doppelgänger," and "Freud's Case-Histories." Some continuity of interests is evident, since older "Freudian" items lead naturally into the four parts which make up "Versions of Baudelaire's Spleen Poems." Here he moves into depiction of life close to the morbid; the images are thrown up by a mind strained and oppressed:

> When earth is changed into an oozing cell
> Where, like a bat in daylight, Hope's frail wing
> Is bruised against the walls, its little skull
> Beating and beating on the leprous ceiling;
>
> When, as the bars of an enormous jail,
> Spread and descend the verticals of rain,
> And a silent race of noisome spiders trail
> Their similar filaments inside one's brain
>
> —And long corteges, with neither drums nor trumpets,
> File slowly through my being. . . .

The unusual "Song Cycle from a Record Sleeve," whose twelve parts consist of prose statements of varying lengths, rather like pensées, express alienation from the ordinary world: "I wonder whether elsewhere there are examples of the lame or out-of-series being accepted by the fit-for-propogation."

Two less personal works continue reflection on the nature of psychic waring. "Apollo on Dionysus," written to mark the centenary of Nietzsche's *The Birth of Tragedy*, recognizes the primary nature of the Dionysian, "understanding/And vindication, both, rise from an art/Riddled with his insanity." The more complex "The Schizophrenics" confronts a radical possibility. The unbalanced may very well provide a damning comment on the so-called normal world which, as is observed, possesses a history of absurdity in any case. A possible truth is that the unusual children who grow up to become the patients who "dream out ... prohibited desires," may really be "the proof of some so far/Frustrated adaptation."

One of a group of garden poems provides an appropriate transition from the preceding, probing an underworld of being to find a calmer regularized life. The catastrophe of "The Catastrophe" is left undefined—possibly the Fall or the industrial revolution or the dropping of atomic bombs or, indeed, all of these—for what really matters in such circumstances is the role of nature, here represented by the birds:

> It was their destiny to guarantee, perhaps
> To man, that after the catastrophe, somehow
> There would survive material evidence of Spring.

There is a particular wit to "The Unremarkable Year," given that its context is such work as the "Spleen Poems" and whatever they imply. While expressing some regret at the possible loss of new stimulation, the speaker sees much merit in a summer with nothing untoward occurring.

> ... There is much to be said for a summer
> Without alarms. The plum crop is modest,
> The monarch has remained unchanged,
> Small differences only in one's teeth and hair and verse-forms.

The title poem "Tiny Tears" is not properly a garden poem since its locale is a beach; yet a doll carcass, the Tiny Tears, could be found in a garden, and its meaning relates to the earlier "The Lawn, Spring and Summer" in which the speaker there finds the body of a baby bird. Finding the doll amid the debris of the seashore—"Strangest fossil in a place of fossils"—leads the speaker into an affirmation of the authentic life represented in his thoughts by procreant woman. The doll symbolizes the ideal models of life men create—noted especially is the doll's "ambiguity/ Of urination"—and their sentimental proclivities "for slightness lost or/ Never possessed." He takes comfort in the fact of the doll's being discarded,

> When the tide goes out, small heads, wristed hands,
> Are left in the wrack among the litter
> Of tougher experiments—comic-book
> Monsters' green hair; pointless ribbons; flora
> From prehistory. Somehow reassuring.

Two poems raise questions concerning the limitations of art. The formal dignity of "Georgic" expresses considerable despair. The great world of "the terrible masters" really has little concern for art; and the artist, in his envy of this world, is likely to make it more dramatic and significant than it actually warrants. But this is not the writer's greatest problem. Since the essential nature of rulers is unchanging, the artist faces the challenge of showing forth by fresh means what has been repeatedly depicted; hence the cry, "what words of mine will show that faces/ Of horses and men are unchanged through history?" The concluding poem, "Homage to Balthus," extends the position. The staggering multiplicity of life shakes the creator's confidence, for no matter what he depicts it will seem "quite pointless in the context of/ possibilities." What further frustrates the artist is his very medium. The "Noble artist" possesses "strange intimations" but these cannot be truly realized because of

> . . . the eternal refusal
> of pigment, canvas, brush to make
> a world parallel to blind creation
> and replace that with its order.

Following as they do "Tiny Tears" these poems indicate the writer's recognition of his own susceptability to the ideal and his ironic capacity to qualify it.[8]

IV   From the Joke Shop

From the Joke Shop is a sequence of sixty-three poems in three-line iambic stanzas widely various in length. The poems are arranged chronologically and run from late summer of one year to the spring of the following one. Most of the poems are discrete but occasionally two or three form a mini-grouping by dealing with a particular situation, for example, a trio about an operation undergone early in the new year.

The typical Fullerian mask is employed throughout, and the subject matter of the poet's personal life is sited in his den, kitchen, garden, and nearby park and shops. The sequence is a summary of familiar themes. The speaker, sixty-two years old he reports, continues to ponder and worry about the state of contemporary culture, his health, his poetry, the local birds, ill health and approaching death, the passing away of close friends, the past—ranging from early memories of his father to wartime experiences—love, and his appearance, now not unlike something from a joke shop. As he says, providing something of a summary of the volume, in "II Kantian Matters":

> And we ourselves have doddered on to odd
> Times and must try for urban philistines
> To make sense out of prosody and dawns.

While it is true that Fuller is not breaking new territory it is clear that the compact, flexible form has proven delightfully stimulating and attests to undiminished creative energy. Anyone familiar with the previous work will be impressed with the sustained ability to play fresh and subtle variations on well established themes. Fuller's garden is truly a place of remarkable poetic fertility.

The year is one in which he is afflicted with insomnia and, accordingly, many of the poems are night pieces, or, after Edward Young, alluded to in one poem, night thoughts. References abound to the authors and books being read to combat sleeplessness, and frequently poems take off from some particular quotation which has stimulated the poet. As well, the matter of dreams, for long a rich source of matter for Fuller, frequently provides subject matter.

A considerable portion of the poems commingle within a single poem a cluster of concerns. Fuller clearly enjoys drawing together apparently heterogeneous matter from the realms of nature, art, and the quotidian and so develop rich tensions between the personal and the universal. "XLIV Cultural History" combines Gombrich on "The mentality of people in a street," the rising price of food, Marx, and the author's bedside notebook. A good instance of the technique is "XXVII Reading at Night about Marcus Aurelius":

> "The gods are always there to show their power.
> They help us humans in their marvellous ways:
> They send us dreams; and they it is provide
>
> The oracles for our uncertainties
> And remedies for our ill-health. In fact,
> They care for us and for our metropoles."
>
> Too *outré* even for an emperor,
> Such words, we think, who've never felt at home
> (nor ever will do) in the universe.
>
> I hope the sparrows roosting in the shrub
> Above my window (presences only leaked
> By droppings on the sill) sleep more than I.
>
> They may include the hen I saw today
> Pick up a small white feather in her bill
> And make herself look like an elderly
>
> Colonel, no doubt retired—as now I am.
> Perhaps the sparrow did it to amuse.
> Perhaps some bird-god does look after us
>
> In such things of no consequence—though I'm
> The last to under-rate the trivial
> Or comic. "Like an ill-roasted egg," I say,

Shifting the ovoid in the simmering pan
As I prepare an early breakfast, struck
With the Swan's penchant for the homely trope.

This is the dismal week when Auden died.
He certainly was hooked up to the gods
As far as we're concerned. Though he himself—

Needing a decent drink, then off to what
More usually was maybe uncertain sleep—
I daresay felt mortal like the rest of us.

And really more than holiness, it's booze
And cigarettes make bearable our lives.
Then cut them short; and leave us to the gods.

This is deceptively casual and achieves a density of impact in a
most unobtrusive way, rather like a disarmingly delicious punch
which holds its fire before suddenly disclosing its unexpected
force. The secret lies in the apparent naturalness of the mind's
movement. In a century which has educated readers to the
strains and leaps of the stream of consciousness this poem is easy
going. Consequently it creates a sense of effortless mental
exfoliation. But in fact the movement is very circumscribed and
not nearly as freewheeling as seems to be the case. The content
shows the speaker to side with Dr. Johnson in his belief that what
counts is the stone that meets the toe. Aurelius's transcenden-
talism is bound to fall rather flat with a nondreaming nonsleeper.
And the concept of universe naturally must leave uneasy such a
mind. More manageable are the birds and, in their mysterious
existence, at least conceivable in a modest way as divine. The
skeptical impulse preserves this possibility and registers too the
dual nature of the birds as perpetrators of droppings and comic
antics, as well as of eggs. The quotation from Shakespeare
reinforces the point of emphasis, the preference "for the homely
trope." The immediacy of Auden's death brings to mind someone
who in one sense had contact with greater powers; but in this
poem his mortality is primary. In an alien universe, faced with
aging and with illhealth and the assurance of death, one can
afford to be honest—undaunted by the certainty of appearing
trivial—and elevate the homely over the holy without losing
sight of the quotidian's duality—amusement or droppings.

Irony, already implied in reference to the title poem where it is accepted that "advancing years" have made superfluous "aids to an amusing appearance," veins the collection. In discussing the book, Fuller speaks approvingly of poetic irony, adding, "For me, the sense of the ludicrous may counterpoint even the most poignant of human affairs; as, in reverse, prosodic regularity helps to authorise the trivial or informal in content and language."[9] Typically, much of the comic irony is directed at the poet himself. A particularly fine instance is in "LIV Winter Solstice" where after ten lines of evocative nature description, the poet asks, "What am I doing in this world of Georgian verse,/ That carries sanguine news?"

One of the volume's strengths derives from the touching nature of the ongoing dialectic carried on indirectly from poem to poem. Moments there are when the speaker feels "Our little lives/Are bad enough without the man-made risk" ("XXI Soldier's Moon"), that the barbarians are not in the future, but now: "Too late to sway the president with art;/Mere plastic pumps, the hearts that might be moved. . ." ("XLVII Waiting for the Barbarians"). But such moments are countered by a great surge of love for life. "VII In Praise of Wakefulness" urges the enjoyment of "the actual":

> The bothersome nights themselves, which after all
> Are ludicrously shorter than the night
> Through which one's sleep will be without flaw.

At the close, the speaker, characteristically, asserts his natural modesty—no expert he:

> It seems to me that after
> Sixty-two Springs I'm still an amateur
> Not just of gardens and wild birds but of
>
> Lived history as well.

And it is this quality of bemused humbleness in the face of the rich variousness of the all, the poet's calm acceptance of his dwindling days, that strikes the volume's deepest, most memorable note.[10]

CHAPTER 5

The Novels

A considerable number of British authors in this century have distinguished themselves in both poetry and fiction. In some instances it is evident a novelist has chosen to write verse—for example, Lawrence and Kingsley Amis—and in others that a poet has chosen to write some fiction—Robert Graves and Philip Larkin. Thomas Hardy represents a case where one hesitates to make an easy distinction, although Hardy saw himself as primarily poet. Roy Fuller views himself as both poet and novelist; his eight novels indicate his seriousness about fiction. As a young man his first creative impulse was toward fiction. He has expressed regret at not writing more fiction in the belief that more chances increase the possibility of greater success. It is noteworthy too that Fuller considers his novel, *My Child, My Sister,* as his best single book, poetry included. However, commendable as is the fiction, and the aforementioned novel in particular, my view is that Fuller the novelist is not of equal stature to Fuller the poet. In poetry Fuller can show a long and distinguished career of subtle and original development; his is a reserved but nonetheless distinctive and valuable poetic voice. Fuller the novelist, once read, seems to fade into the chorus of capable, meritorious, but finally undistinguished novelists with which England in recent decades has been blessed—or, possibly, burdened. A seeming paradox is here evident: on the one hand, novels are easy to write, relatively, and therefore larger numbers of people write them; on the other, the writing of major fiction is so difficult that few achieve real novelistic stature. In the post-Joyce-Lawrence period there is no question that many have been called, but none, seemingly, of first rank.

There are three reasons for welcoming Fuller's fiction. First is the intrinsic worth of the novels; although they break no new ground, anyone who takes pleasure in intelligent well turned fiction will derive pleasure from them. Second, they increase our total sense of the author: the poems display a humanistic outlook of which the novels are realistically conceived embodiments. Third (and this admittedly is largely a question of intuition), the release into fiction refreshed the poet and renewed his poetry.

That Fuller became a better poet in the latter portion of his career is self-evident; that his fiction contributed to this is really undemonstrable. One of the principal distinctions between the earlier verse and the later stems from the increased assurance in the handling of personae. The earlier work is largely dominated by a single persona, and although the later poetry by no means abandons this persona it displays richer subtlizations of it and is more adventuresome in seeking variations. This prompts two guesses about Fuller's ventures into fiction. First, the novels permitted him to escape the persona through which his poetry seemingly had to flow. Interestingly, there are strong familial resemblances between the poetic mask and certain of the later fictional protagonists, as Fuller apparently discovered in fiction as well that he was unable to realize himself creatively without employing what is ostensibly his own artist voice. Second, and this follows from the first and constitutes the principal surmise, the experiences with a cast of fictional characters provided him with the imaginative avenues which enabled him to broaden his conception and handling of his fundamental poetic consciousness.

Fuller, as earlier noted, turned to fiction in the closing stages of World War II when he was at the Admiralty and found the times, for himself, unpropituous for poetry, by writing two children's books, *Savage Gold* (1946) and *With My Little Eye* (1948). The former is an adventure story of a race for gold in Africa between clearly delineated good guys and bad guys. The book's strength is its evocation of place; Fuller of course is taking advantage of his knowledge of Kenya whose landscape had graced many of the poems in *A Lost Season. With My Little Eye* is a teenage crime detection story in which the youthful protagonist helps expose a gang of counterfeiters. This book is a halfway house to the first two adult novels, for both *The Second Curtain* and *Fantasy and Fugue* are versions of the mystery story, and if Fuller followed Graham Greene's categorization of his fictions these would be his "entertainments." In 1966 Fuller wrote the third of his children's books, *Cat's Paw*, done primarily for the then small daughters of his son and meant for a very young audience.

The eight adult novels divide into two unequal groups on the basis of their primary narrative situations, the first six forming one grouping and the last two a second. In a fundamental way the earlier books have a spatial concern, the latter ones a temporal.

Preoccupying Fuller through his first six works is the individual's innocence or unawareness or misreading of his true circumstances even as these begin to enfold and engulf him. Though he lives in a contingent world, man perhaps never loses the capacity for surprise at the nature of the fate which can catch him up and shatter established patterns of routine and habit; he may be staggered to discover hitherto unsuspected adversaries or the extent to which he has been unknowingly manipulated. This concern of the fiction relates to a similar one in the poetry where unease and anxiety frequently assail the speaker. The source of fear, particularly in the earlier poetry, is history itself. Waiting for war to descend and wondering where he will be in a few months time, listening to the bombs whistling down into London, staring into the sea from the rail of a troopship traversing the grey Atlantic, man inevitably pondered the fragility of existence. In transposing this sense to the fictions of more-or-less everyday life in England, domesticating history as it were, Fuller registers the constant tenuousness of human fate.

Taken as a group the six novels, which display resourceful variations on the ambushes of life, record the contrasting results of man's engagement with them. The results can be bad: when an essentially good man is destroyed; they can be good: when a complacent, selfish man gains self-awareness and the capacity to achieve richer relationships. This use of "good" and "bad" should not imply that the novels arrive at tidy and decisive moral conclusions for, in fact, they register the true ambivalence of life caught forever in the living flux.

These novels can be said to possess a spatial dimension because actions taking place and opinions existing at a remove from the protagonist, of which he is totally or largely unaware, prove to exert crucial pressures on his mode of being. But the last two novels, *My Child, My Sister* and *The Carnal Island* are not of this type. Characteristics shared by the first six novels are their minimal use of exposition, indeed their limited need of it, and the relative compactness of lapsed time for the completion of the action (although *The Perfect Fool* is an exception to this second point). But in the latter two books, exposition is all-important. The present action proves to be the completion of a circle of circumstances that have had to wait for some time for the appropriate stimulus for closure. This is the reason for thinking of these novels as temporal rather than spatial.

The last two novels, to paraphrase the title of Fuller's "Poetry of the Final Period," constitute his fiction of the final period not because they are his last novels, but because they echo Shakespeare's final period. A number of late Fuller poems ponder the question of the father's need of or sense of responsibility toward a daughter (possibly emblematic of reconciliation). Both of these books are concerned with the relationships between parents and their children, with the bestowal of blessings upon the younger generation by the older, and with the continuity of the family.

I The Second Curtain

The Second Curtain (1953), cast in the form of an intellectual thriller with a compelling line of action, rises above its form through its protagonist, George Garner, a middle-aged author, publisher's reader, and sometime editor. The novel dramatizes one of the recurring tensions of Fuller's poetry: personal aloofness from life versus the demands of moral involvement. A large, likable, bearded man, not given to much concern with personal appearance, George is an innately private person who, with much initial reluctance, is drawn into a situation which only gradually reveals its magnitude and criminal ramifications.

Early in the book two disparate incidents intrude upon George's obviously insulated existence. First he is offered the opportunity of editing a new literary journal which a wealthy industrialist, Perrott, wishes to launch; and George is surprised at the freedom he would be granted in running the magazine. Next he is appealed to by the sister of an old school friend and longtime correspondent, Widgery, to help her trace his sudden disappearance. Only later, after a series of further unusual incidents, is it possible to discern the connection between the editorship and, as it proves, Widgery's death. Following the apparently accidental death of another man, employed by

Widgery at his small radio components factory, George becomes convinced of the connection. Since everything is viewed from Garner's vantage the reader learns along with him and shares the intensity of incipient threat.

The rightness of his emergent suspicions are confirmed. First there is an attempt to buy him off, and after he rejects this he is followed and eventually given a working over. It is evident he knows too much and is being hounded by an operation that has already killed two men; but the criminal is presented, in this instance, as a virtual student of psychology and economist of violence. Garner seemingly will not be done in because it is adjudged he will be frightened off. The book ends with a trace of ambivalence; but it seems likely Garner, with his smashed mouth, has been deterred.

Garner knows that the enemy is a vague corporate organization concerned with electrical power whose interests were threatened by Widgery's development of "a virtually indestructable filament." If Garner does nothing further it will not be because he lacks courage: this he has demonstrated. It will be for the far more disturbing reason that he feels a sense of helplessness in the face of an amorphous corporate situation. While a few individuals might be apprehended there is a sense that the power source is impregnable. It is evident that a comparison of the book with Graham Greene's earlier entertainments is apt. The corporate force plays the role for Fuller that a vaguely defined foreign power and its agents plays for Greene in his evocation of frightening circumstances. If anything *The Second Curtain* is more disturbing because the events really are closer to home. The book is probably more striking now, twenty-plus years after its publication, with more recent stories of corporate manipulations and political pecadillos of alarming proportions.

From what I have disclosed about the content of the novel, and I have not touched upon many incidents and subsidiary matters, it should be apparent *The Second Curtain* is a good read; but it is more than merely another entertainment by virtue of Garner's characterization which is well in excess of the actual narrative needs. The prose which builds up Garner is richly textured, full of sharp observation, and deftly seasoned with humor. In his subsequent fiction Fuller seldom matched the level of Garner's creation. The vital quality Garner exudes stems from his living out the contradictions of his being: spendthrift habits clashing with sensual inclinations; the disciplined writer at odds with the contemplative idler; the confident literary ego grappling with the mind's uncertainties about its knowledge of life. Garner's thoughts are frequently trial runs for articles and stories he is turning over. Watching the thought processes of the dedicated writer is a pleasurable bonus.

The work is embellished with innumerable little touches that remove it from its generic stereotype. For example, there is a nice little in-joke on entertainments, in effect an apologia for the book. On the occasion of delivering a guest lecture, "Godwin to Greene: the Novel of Pursuit," Garner says in reference to Godwin and *Caleb Williams:* "But when the book was finished he asked himself what he had actually done and was forced to admit that he had only 'written a book to amuse boys and girls in their vacant hours.' In other words, there is, in Godwin's conception and execution of *Caleb Williams,* a writing-down—as there is in the work of all novelists who have chosen to write an 'entertainment' instead of a fully-felt novel"(115).

II Fantasy and Fugue

It is tempting to call *Fantasy and Fugue* not a psychological thriller but a neurotic thriller. The protagonist, Harry Sinton, tells his own story and this makes for Fuller's most highly wrought baroquelike work because Sinton is for most of the novel suffering a nervous breakdown and seemingly headed for mental disintegration. Torn by complex feelings of guilt following the death of his father for which he feels obscurely responsible, Sinton gradually fathoms the source of his condition: he has been systematically manipulated by his elder brother who recognizes the emotional susceptibility of his sibling and exploits it out of jealousy and greed. Like *The Second Curtain,* this novel is developed along the line of pursuit. Both Garner and Sinton must try to construct rational meaning out of apparently disparate rags and tags of incident, driven forward by curiosity and vague suspicions. But *Fantasy and Fugue* is characterized by a breathless, hothouse atmosphere stemming from Sinton's condition, which offers a suspenseful race between the capacity of his rational mind to achieve saving illumination and the increasing threat of a collapse into madness.

Here Fuller has pushed his recurring interest in the divided man—at the intersection of personal desire and moral responsibility—to an extreme. Sinton is burdened with a sense that his involvement with a woman caused him to slight obligations to his father which contributed to the father's death. Sinton's impression of his father's feelings come to him chiefly through his brother who furtively exaggerates. The brother, desirous of possessing both the stately family home and the prestigious family publishing business, has actually killed his father and seems likely to drive his brother to suicide. Coming gradually to the realization that he has been lied to and is being used, Sinton at the close confronts his brother, they grapple, and the brother accidently slips to his death.

This is a highly contrived novel which needs its psychological dimension to work to save it from being merely a momentarily diverting potboiler. The characterization of Sinton and the handling of the first-person narration are experimentally interesting, rather daring actually, but since they do not really function in a convincing way the book finally does not come off. Fuller has kept the book short because, one suspects, he realized that the sustained frenzy of Sinton would prove quickly wearing on the reader. Even so, the effect wears thin all too rapidly. While admiring the attempt, I see this as the least successful novel. Sinton is just too contrived and accordingly the improbability of his situation proves irreparably damaging.

The narration presents a further problem. Instead of having the story told retrospectively, the conventional means of handling such material, Fuller, again daringly, employs the present active tense. The decision obviously was to go for immediacy and to maximize the mystery and to eliminate the sense of Sinton playing with the reader by withholding information. Since the convention is that Sinton is not telling a story he is barred from the kind of preliminary explicitness that would more readily engage the reader. The reader is thus left in the dark about the direction and meaning of Sinton's mental thrashings. But these are not as engaging as they need to be because Sinton is such a cipher. He does not appear worthy of the effort imposed upon the reader and emerges less as a deeply troubled man than as a silly, high-strung adolescent.

The book is not without its fine touches and the best of them is the creation of Rimmer, Sinton's friend, in some ways a reworking of George Garner; but the needs of the book confine Rimmer to two brief appearances.

III   Image of a Society

Since the society in the *Image of a Society* is a building society, the book has as its setting the workings of a corporate entity. This is the one novel in which Fuller has drawn most directly upon his experience as a corporate lawyer, so there can be little question about its essential authenticity. This is a solid, well-crafted book with a necessary largish cast that inevitably offers up stereotypes in several instances. Considered in the context of Fuller's characteristic interests, the book yields additional pleasures.

Image of a Society is reminiscent of C. P. Snow's *The Masters* where competing academic factions seek to gain the election of a particular candidate to the mastership of the college. Here it is the death of the society's manager which creates the issue of his successor. The competition is between the mortgage manager, Blackledge, and the accounts manager, Gerson. The former is outgoing, egotistical, much concerned with public relations, and enamored of the trappings of power; the latter is, quite simply, an emotionless cold fish who serves the corporation like an acolyte. Blackledge begins as the most likely successor and he certainly assumes he will be named; the central story traces out the circumstances of his defeat and the elevation of Gerson.

The machinelike Gerson is involved directly in Blackledge's downfall; but what is interesting is the total lack of personal motivation or competitiveness on his part. Blackledge has involved the firm in an unsound building venture and the dutiful Gerson, with his single-minded and impersonal devotion to figures and to the firm's welfare, is bound to expose this. As the representative of an undoubted type of business-world inhabitant, Gerson is truly frightening. Blackledge, for all his preening is very human, which means, seemingly, that in a business sense he is vulnerable. To the author's credit, Blackledge's death by suicide proves genuinely moving. Blackledge has tried to balance the counterclaims of the stockholders and the self. Perhaps he fails because his ambitions exceed his actual abilities. This view is clearly less distressing than that he was engaged in an impossible task of reconciliation. About this, the book is properly ambivalent.

In *The Masters* in spite of the obvious interest in the outcome of the election, major interest resides in the individual men and what motivates their political manoeuvering and decisions. Similarly, Fuller's primary concern is to explore the impact of the corporate world on particular individuals. The story of Blackledge and Gerson, who both seem true creatures of this world, constitutes approximately half of the canvas. The other half centers on Philip Witt, the society's lawyer, a man who is in the wrong world. Really an aesthetic being hiding behind a businesslike legal exterior, Witt hates his office life. If one question is, who will be named manager? another is, will Witt find the courage to get out? The outcomes balance out, for if Gerson's appointment is, in a humane sense negative, Witt's decision to leave is a positive one. Witt, from the start, appears a weak, indecisive man in his private life, so his portion of the novel traces out the process which enables him to perform what is for him, the courageous act of resignation. Unsurprisingly there is a connection between Blackledge's death and Witt's apparent salvation.

IV   The Ruined Boys

With *The Ruined Boys* (1959) Fuller reached a new plateau in his fiction, for this is mature work of a high order and stands second only to *My Child, My Sister* among the novels. This narrative covering two public school years in the life of Gerald Bracker, is about both victimization through misperception and the destructiveness of the second rate. Replacing the earlier tendency toward melodrama is a subdued, oblique manner of presentation which plays evocatively about the edges of the protagonist's modest daily concerns and scores by its understatement. The subtlety of this reinforces the book's moral dimension which is both guileless and insidious.

Gerald is a sensitive boy, but this is not the conventional schoolboy tale which records the day-by-day misery suffered by such a boy in what often proves to be a brutalizing environment. Gerald can hardly be said to suffer at all and in his own way enjoys his experience. Actually the book is something of a reversal of the convention, for what we come to realize, and Gerald just begins to comprehend, is that Gerald will suffer after he leaves Seaforth House as a consequence of his time there.

When Gerald begins his stay at Seaforth he is awed by the distinguished appearing and aloof headmaster (and owner) Pemberton, a cleric who exudes high moral standards. Gerald, in the intense manner of the preadolescent, determines to emulate him and be worthy of his seemingly high expectations. He suffers real distress when he eventually becomes involved in a minor scrape and is summoned before Pemberton. Feeling he has let the headmaster down, he becomes even more determined to maintain a lofty conception of conduct. His devotion proves to be misplaced; but, since the book is built up with the tiniest of strokes, only gradually does the distance between Pemberton's appearance and his true being emerge. Not until the final scene can the reader really possess the man.

Telling the boys of his great desire to build a chapel for the school, Pemberton launches a campaign to raise funds for it and urges the boys to appeal to their parents. For a time there is a flurry of activity, then there is no further reference to either the chapel or the money realized. The barest hints of financial troubles are dropped and it eventually appears that Pemberton may be in thrall to a local tradesman. The book's very atmosphere depends, of course, on the hidden nature of the world through which Gerald and the other boys move.

During his first year Gerald's best friend is Howarth, a solid outgoing pragmatist, shallow but bright. Significantly, at the end of the year he announces that he will not be back; his parents say, he reports, that Seaforth House is going downhill and thus they prefer to send him elsewhere. This constitutes a turning point—the first evident instance of forewarning—and the completion of the first of the book's two phases.

Given his relatively few appearances, it is notable that Pemberton emerges as complexly as he does. This is achieved by having him viewed imprecisely from largely a child's viewpoint. If he were a calculating man, a deliberate hypocrite, he would, of course, be less frightening. Actually he proves a limited man, a muddled generalist, morally one dimensional and therefore incapable of subtleties of insight. I assume the name of the school, Seaforth, is an ironic comment on the headmaster's weakness. Clearly he cannot see the special boy.

Gerald is a special boy and perhaps even more special is his companion of the second year, Slade. Pemberton can only register that, since Gerald is a year ahead of his friend in school, their relationship is unorthodox and accordingly rather dubious. That they, his most gifted pupils, have been drawn together out of instinctual mutual recognition, is beyond him. In the final scene both boys appear before Pemberton, once more on a negligible breach of regulations. He mishandles them—the weaker instinctively punishing the stronger—and speaks of not being able to give them strong recommendations. Since the boys are already burdened with a modest social background, one is left with the sense that they will be forever at the mercy of the network of which Pemberton is a representative member. More significantly, their conception of the world must suffer distortion as Pemberton and his ways must be assumed by the boys to be the standards by which life is pursued. If one assumes that, but for the social standings of their respective families, Gerald and Slade would have been at a better school where, one would like to think, they would not experience the same handling, it is evident they are doubly damned. One critic has said, "The absolute monarchy of the headmaster in the English public school system has rarely been sniped at with more murderous accuracy."[1]

Another important character is one of the school's younger masters, Percy. A taciturn individual who makes no effort to befriend the boys, Percy does develop a relationship with Gerald after Gerald responds to his playing of the piano and seeks his advice on books to read. Typical of the book's strategy of reticence, the hints which explain Percy's nature are also unobtrusive. It seems evident, however, that he is a Gerald type at a later stage—is, in fact, another of the ruined boys. Percy is not realizing his potential and is clearly burdened with a sense of his mediocre world and his awareness that he is doomed to reside in it. His presence may emblemize the future awaiting both Gerald and Slade.

V   The Father's Comedy

The Father's Comedy, an exemplum against complacency, expresses belief in man's capacity to be selfless. Here love and responsibility disarm pride and ambition. Like George Garner in

The Second Curtain, the protagonist, Harold Colmore, benefits from the slings and arrows flesh is heir to. Colmore is a successful middle-aged business executive in London, self-satisfied and increasingly self-indulgent. A respectable married man with a good address, a taste for luxury cars and expensive cigars, he is finding new stimulation in squiring about a young woman, a friend of his son, whom he is ever ready to explain as "my niece." This is the delusively comfortable state which, in the Fullerian scheme of things, will sooner or later be unsettled by the inevitable workings of a complex social world of human relations. Fuller's book constitutes, of course, a form of literary attack.

From a probing newspaper reporter Colmore learns his son, doing national service, has killed an officer and is under military arrest in an unidentified African country where the British army is involved in peace-keeping duties. Though loath to take an extended leave from his firm for fear his rival will better be able to display himself, Colmore, his wife near hysteria, flies to Africa to comfort his son, investigate the circumstances of the death, and arrange for his son's legal defense. The bulk of the novel covers the African experience. The evocation of the foreign capital in all its heat and seediness is particularly well done. Colmore's immediate discomfort because of his heavy clothing is at once emblematic of the discontinuity of his relations with the community, the army officials with whom he deals, and with his son Giles.

For Colmore nothing is to prove easy. His first meeting with Giles is frustrating because communication is made difficult by his initial insensitivity. However, though shaken by various early experiences, Colmore is basically too poised and self-controlled not to cope and gradually adjust. Just as he purchases and adopts proper clothing, so too he begins to get in touch with circumstances.

Giles, it emerges, was arousing suspicion among his officers even before his encounter with the one he is accused of murdering, so that the crime is being associated with his seeming revolutionary proclivities. Giles had become involved with a group of native dissidents, and this, coupled with Gile's barrack-room reading of Marx, causes the army to judge him a dangerous element. The heart of the novel is the revelation of Colmore's reaction to his son's humane response to the native population. The story that finally emerges in a forceful courtroom sequence is this: Giles criticized his superior because he was manhandling a native. The angered officer drew his revolver, Giles reacted by pushing him, and in falling the officer inadvertently shot and killed himself. Giles is acquitted on the grounds of self-defense. What is of greater interest is Colmore's courtroom conduct. Colmore determines to tell the court of his own Marxist leanings years previous and that Giles's involvement with Marx started when he found his father's old books put aside in the attic. Colmore does this although legal counsel points out that such testimony is unnecessary and although he realizes his revelation, bound to be well publicized in the British press, will doubtless block any further advance in his career. His testimony thus is a measure of his renovation, a way of solidifying his new relationship with his son, and possibly an act of contrition for his previous attitude and conduct, and a way as well of acknowledging an earlier, perhaps better self.

We are not likely to disagree with Fuller's moral stance; the outcome is right, but predictable and bland. *The Father's Comedy* reads well but does not reverberate once the cover is closed.

VI   The Perfect Fool

The Perfect Fool (1963) is the longest and most ambitious of the novels. In one sense the protagonist, Alan Percival, is a victim of his natural appearance, his upbringing, and his moment in history. In another sense his is the fate of all human beings. At one point Percival is linked with the character Parsifal, described as "the blameless fool, made wise through pity." This may be viewed as a cryptic summing up of Percival's journey in the novel. In many ways the consequence of time and circumstance, Percival's personal freedom can best fulfill itself in his accepting responsibility for his actions and rejecting the obvious temptation of bitterness in favor of a general compassion.

The novel covers the first thirty or so years in Percival's life during the period 1912 to 1947. Two of the six chapters show him as a child, the third as a novice journalist of twenty, the fourth as a wartime serviceman, the fifth as a married journalist in postwar London, and the brief sixth, on his own after being left by his wife. Since Fuller was born in 1912 and went through a version of several of Percival's experiences, one assumes considerable parallelism, although this is clearly not an autobiographical novel. For instance, Percival is born in the Midlands, loses his father at eight, is in the radar branch of the Royal Navy, serves in Africa, and is eventually recalled to England, all of which corresponds to Fuller's own life.

Percival's childhood is highly determinative of the adult he becomes. When he is eight he loses not only his father but undoubtedly a particular life-style, for his father's death occurs shortly after he has started to succeed to the point where he has acquired a chauffer-driven limousine. A short time later Percival loses his mother in childbirth and is consequently raised by aged grandparents in quiet circumstances. In the face of all this the child, rather admirably, is determined to conduct himself as if nothing untoward has occurred. He continues

to play for all he was worth the conception that his circumstances were no different from anyone else's. . . . It seemed to him most necessary to prove to others that his being selected as fate's victim perturbed him not the least—nor must it inspire in *them* any sense of guilt or pity. Again, since his life prior to his father's death had been safe and uneventful he believed that those were the proper characteristics of all life which it behoved him to continue to have applied to his own.

Both this outlook and his life-style conspire to make Percival a basically retiring and unaggressive individual, which is why his wife Ann eventually leaves him. Percival emerges at twenty into a self-conscious innocent socially unskilled and possessed of contradictory tensions. On the one hand, he feels himself to be special, somehow singled out (he feels he is searching for the grail his Arthurian namesake sought), and he knows he is possessed of a handsome face. On the other hand, he is afflicted with a sense of unworthiness and inadequacy. It is his face that makes him the object first of homosexual advances which startle him, and later the attentions of his future wife.

Wartime experience simply underlines Percival's noncompetitive nature. Because he is unassertive the advancement his natural talent warrants is slow coming. But eventually his career develops, doubly blessed because the attractive Ann Best, the most desired girl on the base where Percival is undergoing advanced training, is drawn to him by what she identifies as his mystery. One suspects that, in circumstances other than service life, Percival would not have had the opportunity to marry Ann.

In London after the war Percival finds himself in rather enviable circumstances, possessed of a beautiful wife whom he worships and writing for the prestigious weekly, *The New Watchman.* His bliss is short-lived. Ann, who works for a large building society, become enamored of money and power and accordingly of the men who are hustling to exploit the fiscal opportunities afforded by the postwar situation. She is delighted when she discovers that a cousin of Percival's is a member of Parliament with a significant post in the Labour government and through her husband helps her new friends get at the relative. Percival, who does not share Ann's ambition and is in fact of long-standing socialist persuasion, eventually balks, though even so he comes off looking pathetic, for his cousin assures him that given his political position he is the constant recipient of attention from entrepreneurs who wish to have inside information on real estate matters. Realizing that, in her terms, Percival is a nonstarter, Ann leaves him for one of the postwar hustlers.

The book's conclusion creates a sense that hitherto Percival's life has been a captured existence, that unbeknown to him he had simply been preparing to love. So his search for the grail has been for the moment when he came into possession of his life. He has made contact with a young woman who, significantly, bought the seat at the opera which originally was destined for Ann. Percival thinks she may not find him "exasperating, and that in his turn he might come to find of greater interest her naive but knowledgeable mind. . . ." She constitutes something of a mirror image of Percival and in this sense suggests that Percival has at last found himself.

The Perfect Fool is an intriguing idea and soundly written; but it remains merely a good novel and not the major novel it might have been. The problem is inherent perhaps in the conception of Percival. He is always dominated by the people and circumstances who surround him and in which he has his being. Fuller has thus produced an interesting if obviously circumscribed social history of a particular historical period; but this does not mean he has solved the problem of making a rich and satisfying creation out of an intentionally limited central character.

VII   My Child, My Sister

My Child, My Sister is Fuller's finest novel and one deserving of recognition for its movingly achieved insights into human

relations and motivations. The protagonist and narrator is Albert
Shore, a sixty-year-old successful novelist, a witty as well as
thoughtful observer and commentator on life, and one especially
alert to his own penchants and foibles. Since his creatively tuned
mind tends to be fascinated by the relationship between art and
life and he frequently examines experience in the light of its
viability for fictional treatment, we have the added experience
of seeming to enter directly into the primary workshop of the
active writer. Shore's concern for art and his involvement with
the artistic community and his penchant for aperçus provide a
rich matrix for the foreground narrative action.

The student of Fuller is bound to note a paradoxical fact about
My Child, My Sister. As suggested earlier, one reason Fuller may
have turned to fiction was as a means gaining release from the
pervasive poetic persona which his poetry seemingly required.
Yet in this, his finest fiction, he has created in Shore essentially
the characteristic mask of the poetry. To run from one's fate may
be the more readily to confront it; in any case Shore remarks at
one point, "I think how fate always makes use of events intended
to avoid it" and this may strike us as apt in this context. Shore in
characterizing his art as "sane" and "mandarin," and in such
thoughts as "I simply wonder how I qualify to be an artist in a
world inimical to art" appears privy to Fuller's own views. But
this is all to the good and is the basis of the book's success. It is
Shore's mind that is literally and figuratively the book.

In the simplest terms *My Child, My Sister* is about the ongoing
process of loss and gain, and employs two separate though
closely related stories to convey this. The initial story concerns
the marriage of Shore's son Fabian and the book ends with Shore
sitting in his son's garden playing with the child with which the
marriage has been blessed. Shore's acquisition of a daughter-in-
law and a granddaughter is, however, only a portion of his gain.

When Fabian first tells his father that he wishes to marry
Frances Leaf, Shore is brought up short because Frances's
stepmother, Eve, is Fabian's mother, the woman Shore divorced
twenty years previous following her involvement with
Christopher Leaf who was at the time a student of Shore's, then
an Oxford tutor. Even though Shore had his way in gaining the
right to raise Fabian, and although he went on to live happily
with Blanche common law for many years prior to her death,
Shore still carries the pain and consequent acrimonious feelings
of Eve's betrayal. Shore is disturbed by his son's news and thinks,

"Could it really be that this long sterile epoch of my life of 'hatred and rancour' would have to be ended?" (29). The answer in due course is yes—all reservations wiped out on both sides by Frances's announced pregnancy—and both Shore and the Leafs make inroads of insight into what the other side has been feeling over the years. The marriage salves the old injuries, at least on the social level. True personal contact, when it comes later, comes for another reason.

The second, more important, more moving, story results from Shore's involvement with the Leaf's teenage daughter, Flip. Mutual interest in the creative—Flip is an art student—facilitates their initial rapport. Shore's feelings for Flip are complex: she is the daughter he never had; he is both touched and troubled by her profound sadness and belittling of herself. Shore's early remarking, "You could have been my daughter," is echoed later by Flip who asks, "could you in some way be my father?" Flip proves to be the story's element of loss. As Fabian and Frances flourish so Flip slips further into a private hell which leads at first to stays in a private nursing home, but eventually, perhaps permanently, to confinement in a state mental institution. Flip is thus an aspect of the inexplicable intransigence in life. At first she is spoken of as eccentric; then Fabian suggests that her moods are a consequence of her having been rather squashed by her mother. Clearly these explanations are inadequate and simplistic, and the book makes no attempt to provide much more in the way of explanation. Flip herself believes that her father wanted a son in place of her, and she has a fixation that he wishes to kill her. The sad truth is, she does not respond to treatment. Shore has had early intimations that Flip's troubles ran deep. On the only occasion when Flip shows Shore her strange paintings he thinks of them as "symptoms or messages—cries for help, perhaps." Leaving her the same evening he feels he is "leaving her to deal with the frightful details of a final illness. ..."

Shore's faithful visits to Flip's sickroom recall his care of Blanche throughout her terminal illness, his continuous concern for Fabian, and his nursing of a baby starling at the time Eve left him permanently. Though acts surely of love, Shore understands them in different terms: "Not affection or curiosity drives me on, but the will to succour essential animal life ... which in me is never habitual, but must always be exercised afresh in the face of fear, repugnance, morbid pity—though as the years pile up one more clearly recognizes, breaking the initial barrier, the actions to be taken, the pain to be suffered, and so a kind of habit is established after all." This statement is central to the novel and is also significant as an insight into Fuller's motivation as a writer. Shore is obviously not a passionate man (presumably one reason why Eve left him for Christopher), displaying reserve in both life and art; but this does not invalidate his concern for vital living. In fact, Shore's principle of dispassionate passion can be seen repeatedly in various situations as particularly inimical to the conduct of cordial interaction. *My Child, My Sister* thus may be viewed as an apologia for a particular approach to life. In a sense it is a reaffirmation of the old adage, a lean horse for a long race.

The book opens with the words "A baby cried in the distance." Shore at once is nonplussed, for he is sitting in the dining room of his London club. He ponders the explanation of what he has heard, but when the noise recurs he locates its origin: "I realized that it came from my chest. ...." This is a provocative touch, typical of many such in the novel, which leads along several suggestive lines through the book. There is the concern for relations between parents and children; the question of the responsibility of the strong for the weak; and the recognition of the infantile facets of the self (for instance, Shore's involuntary voyeurism). The baby within may be what Shore terms the eternal will for survival and renovation.

The image of an offspring returns in the closing scene. Shore, visiting Fabian and Frances, is sitting in their garden entertaining their daughter Freda. First she wishes to play "not very well today" which game discloses that her Poohbear "wasn't very well today yesterday." The reiteration of the theme of illness or loss is balanced by the little story Shore tells Freda about a little girl establishing peace between Snake and Bear. As the child urges her grandfather on he responds with what he characterizes as "his failing but ever-eager powers to fresh feats of human love and creative insight," meanwhile musing, and correctly so, that his theme is "renewal, optimism, life. ...."

VIII   The Carnal Island

Fuller's fascination with the writer as protagonist, previously evident in George Garner of *The Second Curtain* and Albert

Shore in *My Child, My Sister,* comes to a climax in *The Carnal Island* where the two principal characters are both poets. In the two earlier books the artist and his concern were subordinate to other narrative matters; but in *The Carnal Island* the life of the artist, the relationship between art and life, the function of art in society, and such corallary themes, are central. Too, the book has a dimension of nuance available to those familiar with Fuller's career.

This is a short novel, more a novella, possessed by a single unfolding line of development and a marked use of lietmotiv. The narrator, James Ross, a young, unestablished poet who works for a London publisher, is invited to visit the distinguished elder poet, Daniel House (who himself worked for a publishing firm years previous) on the south coast of England, ostensibly to discuss an anthology House might prepare. The story that unfolds contains considerable dramatic irony that discloses itself only later in the book.

Beneath the realistic narrative surface one comes to recognize the configurations of a myth about the artist. The aged House, who dies at the end, is actually engaged in setting his house in order by assuring that what he represents is to be sustained by the neophyte James. James can be said, I believe, to inherit House's muse. The action covers two days and on the first, the day James arrives from London, the atmosphere is restrained, the tone set by House's younger, formal wife. This first day is perhaps properly viewed as a test for James, to determine his worthiness for a further journey. Neither James nor the reader really graps at first the significance of certain of House's comments. For instance, harking back to their only previous meeting in London, House says, "I was quite on tenterhooks that eventually you'd say something foolish. Or, rather, something that would show we weren't on the same beam after all." The introduction of a neighboring poet at dinner serves to establish the closeness of the kinship between House and James. For one thing, it becomes evident James is in touch with the core of reality in life from which the third poet holds himself aloof.

The novella centers on the journey of the second day. House takes James across water aboard an ancient ferry to the island which James realizes is the very island enshrined in House's early and most famous collection of poems entitled *The Carnal Island.* James is touched by a stirring sense of premonition: "For the first time I felt the unease of being propelled into another's intimate affairs." On the island James is led to a small house to meet, first, House's middle-aged illegitimate, unmarried daughter Margaret, and then, Margaret's illegitimate teenage daughter Jan. Jan informs James eventually of the uniqueness of his visit: "He's never brought anyone over here before. . . ." Before the day of visiting is over a strong mutual attraction has been shared by James and Jan.

On the return journey the death which has been repeatedly hinted at occurs: the old ferry sinks and, although James is able to swim to shore towing House, the experience is too much for the old poet's heart. Later, recuperating in hospital, James thinks: "It seemed that in a way House's death, more than his living might have done, possessed the power to link me with his carnal island." Exactly. Though the book says nothing beyond this about the future, the sense of succession is pervasive.

While it would be inappropriate to speak of *The Carnal Island* as autobiographical, it is nevertheless the most personal of Fuller's fictions in its portraits, opinions, and manner of expression. The relationship between the youthful James and the older House takes on a particular coloration in the light of this comment by Fuller during the course of a recent interview:

I've been very fortunate in having my son during the last fifteen years or so to read most of my stuff; I've always relied enormously on his judgment. If I hadn't had him, I think probably I would have wanted much more to find some congenial, preferably younger writer in London to consult. This is enormously helpful to a writer and I think far too many English writers just go on relying on their own judgment, not taking stock of the generations coming up below them. I know it's difficult to establish contact in that way, and I've been particularly fortunate, I think.[2]

The discussions which James and House have on the nature and function of the artist and his relationship to his times clearly afford Fuller an opportunity to explain views that are quite evidently his own, for they are views which appear, less overtly, in the verse and in the criticism. A considerable list of cross references could be compiled, but a few instances will suffice by way of illustration. James and House briefly discuss an essay by Wallace Stevens, a poet who becomes the subject of one of Fuller's Oxford lectures. There are references to the thirties and to Spain (which House had visited), to Marx and to Freud. Some descriptive touches are characteristic Fuller poetic lines presented in prose: "In a tree nearby starlings were carrying on their subdued autumnal chummering, argumentative domesticity having replaced the shrill ecstasies of summer love." Some of Fuller's comments are virtually private jokes because they comment on aspects of his own career as a poet: "The poetic persona I used to assume was always much older than my real age . . . ." or, "If only one's art hadn't always to be ironical. . . ."

Given the author's long-standing concern with the impact of fate or the impact of the casual upon the individual life this book is of special interest. The intrusion of the unexpected is evident enough if we consider the effect of his visit upon James and certainly the breakup of the ferry and the consequent death of House appear sufficiently happenstantial. At the same time there is a powerful sense of man's capacity to manage or at least acquiesce in a kind of inevitable destiny. House, because he has chosen and initiated James, has as it were invited death; James, because he has accepted House's invitation, has tacitly agreed to become heir to House's power. The artist, in this myth, thus partakes of the autonomy of the world of art and while subject to the immutable laws of nature (aging, death, recurrence) rises above the quotidian flux. With this novel it may be said Fuller's prose fiction flowed naturally back into the main channel of his poetry.[3]

CHAPTER 6

The Criticism

THE bulk of Roy Fuller's criticism consists of literary journalism, chiefly book reviews. Since the late thirties he has contributed hundreds of items to such staple English publications as *The Listener, The Times Literary Supplement, London Magazine, Encounter,* and *The New Statesman.* His one sustained commitment was as *The New Statesman's* television critic in 1966 and 1967. The culmination of his critical activities came with his election as professor of poetry at Oxford in 1968, the consequent lectures being published in two volumes, *Owls and Artificers* in 1971 and *Professors and Gods* in 1973.

Common sense marks this criticism expressed in informal conversational prose which often incorporates personal experiences. This is criticism that does not raise its voice, preferring to sustain a good-natured reasonableness. Not that one can remain in doubt about Fuller's continuing advocacy of high standards and insistence that writers demonstrate honest labor in their art. Fuller has enjoyed a reputation in recent years for being something of the conscience of English writing.

I Owls and Artificers

Three of the lectures in *Owls and Artificers* are directly concerned with forces that contribute to depressed cultural conditions. Appropriately the first lecture, "Philistines and Jacobins," invokes Arnold's *Culture and Anarchy.* Fuller says, "I want to see how his century-old ideas stand up, and in particular to apply some of his useful and imaginative terminology to the conditions of to-day." Fuller concludes that the Philistine notions which Arnold attacked have entrenched themselves even more deeply. Troubling as this is, Fuller, writing at a time of student foment, adds, "what is disturbing is that youth's rebellion is not

125

specifically against the spreading Philistinism that Arnold so
clearly saw as a concomitant of the spread of affluence but
indeed is often productive itself of Philistinism of another kind."
    Basically Fuller wants to see two things happen. First, critics
who can fulfill "criticism's primary task, that of telling us
whether the work of art under consideration is any good or not."
The second desire is more basic and more complex. Expressing
sympathy with Arnold's "democratic idea," Fuller says, "surely
history proves that the horse of social change must be put before
the cart of cultural enlightenment." This very convincingly
establishes the consistency of Fuller's fundamental position
dating from the thirties.
    Both "'Woodbine Willie' Lives!" and "How to Stuff Owls" are
concerned with kitsch. The former lecture reminds us that while
poetic claptrap dates quickly to reveal its true nature, it can fool
the unwary when fresh and "dressing itself fashionably." The
characteristics of sentimentality in poetry are examined and then
several instances of contemporary verse that have "a veneer of
modernity" are given a litmus test which reveals deformations in
both feeling and language. A typical Fuller touch is his wry
comment about the failure "to go through the business of
grinding the beans and getting out the percolator."
    "How to Stuff Owls," taking off from the old anthology of bad
verse, *The Stuffed Owl*, suggests the categories employed by the
editors of good "bad" verse and bad "bad" verse might better be
replaced by those of harmless bad verse and dangerous bad
verse. The former is characterized as work "unlikely to be
admired or imitated." Since it is dangerous bad verse, of course,
which is really of concern, the essay principally pursues its
attributes. The basis of bad verse is "crude sensibility" which
manifests itself in three categories— "technical misconceptions,
inaccurate expression and unobservant feeling." Fuller is
especially troubled by a present-day element of antiintellectual-
ism and antitraditionalism. He reminds that "our own experience
confirms above all else ... that mere feeling is too easy," and
concludes, "surely it is only by entering into the tradition,
amplifying and (if we are usually talented) extending it, that our
own sensibilities can be properly expressed." Following the
example of *The Stuffed Owl* editors, Fuller declines to quote
instances of bad verse in living poets—characteristically he
quotes some of his own work—and concentrates on two noted

English poets, Blake and Lawrence, who are, in his view, poets capable of both splendid work and work that is "bombinating," "flabby," or "indulgent." Verse by both poets is examined and found to be dangerous. Fuller is concerned that all of Blake, for example, will be admired and the bad parts of it employed as models as readily as the good.

Syllabic versification is investigated in "An Artifice of Versification," primarily by considering the practices of Elizabeth Daryush and Marianne Moore. Though technically oriented, the essay does give the uninitiated a whiff of the poet's workshop, and by the close one concurs with Fuller that "whatever the extent to which English prosody may admit new rules, new practices—one thing is certain: there is nothing particularly simple about the way good poems are fabricated." It is the "extreme formal element" in syllabic verse that provides "confidence in its validity" for Fuller, who quotes with approval Allen Tate's insistence that "Formal versification is the primary structure of poetic order, the assurance to the reader and to the poet himself that the poet is in control of the disorder both outside him and within his own mind."

Fuller begins "The Filthy Aunt and the Anonymous Seabird" by considering, "from the poet's point of view—what minimum understanding he asks from his reader and, *per contra,* what his obligations may be to remove possibilities of misunderstanding." Briefly, he regards the latter question first: the poet should insure both the soundness of the poem's "internal logic" and the truth of the poem's details, since "the total meaning of the poem often resides in its details. . . ." As for the reader, he must willingly accept "the work-task the poet legitimately imposes," since this "is all part . . . of the poem's effect." Fuller sets up three categories of readers and a heirarchy of the poet's hopes, linking, naturally, the greatest hope to the entire readership: "In the long run . . . the poet would consider it vital for the reader to comprehend completely his central theme; he would also like, but not think it essential, for his external references to be picked up. What might be called the poem's internal references—its logic, its prosodic effects, its connections back and forth—the poet would be confident that some readers some day would tumble to them."

The essay affords Fuller an opportunity to attack that professional criticism—with its "crack-pot speculation" and "magical mumbo-jumbo"—which at worst causes the poem to disappear or at least become blurred. For Fuller, "exhaustive commentary is self-defeating. . . ." After noting several striking (or horrifying) instances of pompous misreadings, Fuller singles out one of his great predecessors as Oxford professor of poetry, A. C. Bradley, as an exemplar critic performing the duties of the intermediary between poet and reader in an intelligent and judicious manner, and a typical example of his poised working method is examined. Bradley is able "to perform a truly critical function" by his "lack of dogmatism and the presentation of the alternatives. . . ."

"Both Pie and Custard" is a tribute to Wallace Stevens. Fuller's initial interest is readily understandable, for here is another lawyer who successfully combined corporate and artistic careers. Fuller expresses both delight and admiration for Stevens's letters which compose "one of the great books of the twentieth century." But as the essay makes clear, the regard for Stevens is not founded on the fact of a parallel career so much as on a shared world view. Two or three quotations will quickly establish points of contact between the poets, and Fuller's sympathies are readily understandable since the American's views indirectly constitute approbation of Fuller's own motivations as poet. "This equating of poetry with reality, however tentative, I find very moving." Again, "The essential alienation of man from the universe is a constant theme of Steven's own verse. . . . But for Stevens the alienation is the source, not the daunting, of poetic creativity. . . ." And finally:

As Stevens says later in "Notes Toward a Supreme Fiction", the task is "not to console/Nor sanctify, but plainly to propound." It follows from all this, I think, that the long series of Stevens's poems is sustained by the conviction that poetry's apprehension of reality alone gives meaning to existence, while the poetry is saved from aestheticism or from anything else smacking of the high falutin by a sombre and indeed pessimistic sense of the terrible and uncaring realities behind the skies and trees observed by the poet with so much accuracy and love.

"Both Pie and Custard," the finest of the *Owl and Artificer* essays, is thus doubly valuable, offering a succinct, penetrating consideration of the understructure of Stevens's poetry, as well as affording true insight into Fuller's personal artistic biases.

II   Professors and Gods

The first three essays of *Professors and Gods,* subtitled *Last Oxford Lectures on Poetry,* examine the relationship between art and science and especially as the latter affects poetry. In "The Radical Skinhead" Fuller reopens the controversy of C. P. Snow and F. R. Leavis on culture. While paying tribute to Snow's generous outlook and conduct, Fuller argues that his concept of the two cultures is "unreal or unmeaningful." He offers two counter arguments. First, "There is not just one literary culture," so that the scientist, as with any man, is "at the mercy of the men of letters who dominate the organs of literary opinion. ..." Second, "when culture is under fire its indivisible nature is apparent, and its separation into the literary and the scientific no more than a matter of mere terminology." Although he has reservations about aspects of Leavis's position, Fuller finds it has "enormous appeal." Noting the hate lavished on Leavis from many quarters of the cultural establishment, Fuller explains that "the ruling literary culture" is always "a middlebrow" one whose "standards and calibre fall short of the best the age can confer." Accordingly it is the severity of Leavis's demands which unsettle this culture. Fuller is further troubled by contemporary elements which, though attacking middlebrow culture, have no sympathy either with the tradition of cultural achievement of which Leavis is the champion. What Fuller comes to argue for is essentially Matthew Arnold's clerisy or saving remnant, and he issues a rallying call: "isn't there, in the possibility of merely a comparatively few holding on to standards, discovering and perhaps continuing 'the great tradition' of English literature, isn't there in this a ground for hope?" This is the most forceful of all of the Oxford lectures and the most deserving, rather the most needful, of wide circulation.

"The Orbicularity of Bulbs" examines in some detail Aldous Huxley's views in *Literature and Science* and certain of his essays— Huxley being of special interest as a figure with a foot in both spheres—and, more briefly, Christopher Caudwell's *Studies in a Dying Culture.* Fuller more readily approves of Caudwell, though conceding Huxley's value in contributing to the return of thirties poetry to a greater openness to science than that of previous decades. Fuller reiterates that "Without the

scientific respect for and examination of reality any poetic
movement towards colloquilism of diction or freedom of form
seems doomed to end in mere rhetoric and sentimentality or
vapidity." Ire is expressed over certain present tendencies:

> The extreme violence, of imagery and ideas, of some contemporary
> poetry goes beyond any attempt to depict, to grapple with, our present
> woes: it seems likely, rather, to add to those woes by providing their
> mere artistic mimicry. I've never been able to see why art, in the face of
> chaos, feels that it must itself be chaotic.

Fuller quotes with approval what Auden had to say in *A Certain
World* about the two cultures controversy: "What the poet has to
convey is not 'self-expression,' but a view of reality common to
all, seen from a unique perspective, which it is his duty as well as
his pleasure to share with others." For Fuller the poet and
scientist "have essentially the same purpose—the delineation
and amelioration of the real world."

Pursuing the Leavisite one-culture thesis, "The Osmotic Sap"
continues Fuller's ongoing discussion about poets remaining in
touch with reality. Though poetic success is not insured by the
poet's casting "about in some scientific stream ... a blind or
neutral attitude to science tends to insulate the poet from the
spirit of his age and narrows his apprehension of reality. . . ."
Poets are, in fact, "more concerned with accuracy" than critics
generally allow. A parallel is found between poets and scientists:
"Both poetry and science are international." This provides a
form of guarantee for "there are in science and poetry standards
of truth that can't be abandoned and that essentially never have
been abandoned."

The proximity of problems facing modern poets and novelists
is the subject of "The Two Sides of the Street." Henry James's
seemingly paradoxical insistence, in the words of the critic
Laurence Bedwell Holland, "that the novel was the most
intimate of forms," and accepted by Fuller as true, is one of the
several nodes instanced where poetry and the novel touch.
Another concerns what Fuller calls "the nose-picking element"—those mundane human activities which normally contribute to fiction's verisimilitude and also constitute "a counterpoint . . . to the higher themes of life which the novel" deliniates,
but which gained entrance into modern poetry especially
through Eliot. Fuller also considers the implication of novels

being characterized as "poetic." More significant, finally, are the distinctions between poet and novelist, and these are succinctly epitomized by adapting some words from Nietzsche's *The Birth of Tragedy*: "in the novel Dionysus must speak in the language of Apollo; in poetry, in the last analysis, Apollo uses the tongue of Dionysus."

"Fascinating Rhythm" deals with what the author calls "this baffling prosodic subject." While admitting that rhythm is by no means the most interesting element in poetry, Fuller says it "is the root of the matter," while implying one of the limiting factors in contemporaneous verse is insufficient grasp of the subtleties of rhythm: "The poet's work as interpreter of his life and his age has always gone on alongside, as part of, his work as metrist—a truism which perhaps would only need to be uttered in a time of debased, metrical standards." Thomas Campion in particular is held up as an exemplar of "individual rhythm" and certain of his practices examined. Driving home the importance of his topic Fuller makes this most intriguing and enlightening comment: "one's whole experience as a poet brings home to one that what prevents a poet from being a poet all the time—the business of inspiration—is not so much the lack of ideas or perceptions as the trickiness of casting them into rhythmical form."

"Professors and Gods" sustains Fuller's attack against the barbarian tendencies of modern culture. Drawing again upon the Nietzschian split between Apollo and Dionysus he argues that much recent art regretably has elevated Dionysus and largely dispensed with Apollo. This has led to distortions and loss of balance for, "The operant forces have not changed . . . the savant and the layman, the professor and the god, paleface and redman, Apollo and Dionysus. Truly civilized man has to play both roles but . . . in one person. And art should be a reflection of that tricky unity—a unity not of opposites but of the potentials in human nature and human society." Fuller supports Leavis's view "that great art is necessarily impersonal," and considers the achievement of impersonality particularly in the poetry of commitment. For Fuller, "All poetry . . . must earn the values it intends to subsist by," though, of course, "the quality of its work" must refine perception "in the interests of truth" so that "the merely ideological" is transcended. Attention is also drawn to the influx of the half-educated into the ranks of creative artists, those who often favor the presentation of strong emotion by a direct method. By quoting from the French critic Julien Benda's book *Belphegor,* chiefly written before 1914, Fuller notes that the modern antihuman elements abroad have been at work for decades. If one did not know otherwise one would surmise, at least from the passages quoted by Fuller, that Benda was surveying the contemporary scene.

Fuller turns to recent poetic history for two of his lectures. Although "English Poetry of the Two World Wars" centers upon the work of Siegfried Sassoon and Wilfred Owen from the first war and that of Keith Douglas and Alun Lewis from the second, and characterizes the differences in the work resulting from the distinctive wars and traces out the causes of the differences, the work is ultimately a tribute to all of the war poets:

Preparing this lecture ... I've been moved not only by the waste of talent but also by the reiteration by so many poets, often scarcely out of their boyhood, of the essential brotherhood of mankind, and of the brotherhood, too, of poets and their audience. What a marvellous and tragic literature this is, the best of it; in the end beyond critical carping and judicious placing, reflecting the human spirit that we hope—that we must believe—will rescue us from the disasters inherent in history and the outworn systems in which we are shackled, from all the ways that, in Owen's words, "nations trek from progress."

Since Fuller's poetical-political consciousness blossomed with and because of the early thirties, "Poetic Memories of the Thirties," holds particular interest for the student of Fuller or of that decade's poetry. The essay conveys something of the early excitement of the young Fuller reading the freshly minted work of Auden in *Poems* (1930) and of Stephen Spender, among others, in *Oxford Poetry* (1930). This is a wide ranging essay as Fuller considers the verse which such poets as Auden and Spender later revised or omitted from their collections, the relationship of poetry to politics, the technical inheritance from Pound and Eliot, the primary groupings of poets, the arrival of the surrealist element in the middle of the decade, and, of course, a good dollop of personal reminiscence. In Fuller's view no work captures or is more essential to an understanding of the period than Edward Upward's two novels, *In the Thirties* and *The Rotten Element.* Fuller concludes by underlining the continuity between the earlier period and the present: "Nor has the prime requirement of the Thirties really changed, so far as poets feel in their bones that poetry ought somehow to be in the service of ... humanity, and that politics should be as truthful as poetry."

In his final lecture, "The Planet on the Table," Fuller proceeds "cautiously round the circumference of" Shakespeare, noting "it seemed rather bad that during" his five years at Oxford he had not previously mentioned the Bard. Profferring no thesis, the author touches upon assorted topics which have concerned him over the years, such as: good and bad Shakespearean criticism (he especially commends Alice Walker's *Textual Problems of the First Folio* and E. K. Chamber's *William Shakespeare: A Study of Facts and Problems*); how actors misspeak the verse and how it might best be managed ("In general, a much slower, more thoughtful and less emotional delivery is to be recommended, with the easier effects of pathos and comedy strictly avoided.") Rather humorously he relates his one venture into Shakespearean scholarship: tracking down the origin of the word "Andrew," the vessel Salario refers to in the opening scene of *The Merchant of Venice*. Leavis's insistence that Shakespeare is no mandarin is reasserted and approved. The concluding statement is addressed directly to students and it is fitting these summary words be quoted:

And perhaps the lesson is conveyed that going down eventually from here, from the life of emotional experience set among books and many other trophies of culture, into a world and an age on the whole inimical to such things, need not mean an utter abandonment of the striving for standards, and for the better understanding of the old and the new in literature, our notable and idiosyncratic poetry in particular.

CHAPTER 7

Conclusion

L ITERARY history will almost certainly record that Roy Fuller was one of the handful of Englishmen who sustained the quality of British poetry during the relatively lean period from 1950 to 1960. George MacBeth has suggested with both humor and astuteness that Fuller was somewhat unlucky in the timing of his career. In the thirties he was too young and had written too little poetry to really be counted among the full-fledged members of Auden's army; though he wrote more first-rate poetry during the war years than any other Englishman, the war did not kill him and hence sanctify this work with an aura of great loss; and though he performed with the virtues of the Movement poetry of the fifties, he was not a fresh face and hence did not stimulate the kind of excitement which greeted the pristine Larkin, Amis, and Gunn among others. This is not the kind of record to trouble Fuller. The early thirties coloration of his earlier work has been proven to be rather deceptive; though of his time, Fuller has marched to his essentially independent beat. While many of the poets who caused a greater stir in the fifties and sixties than did Fuller have either ceased writing verse or been unable to sustain their first promise, Fuller with undiminished productivity and quality has never broken pace.

It is easy enough to note what Fuller has not done. In his period he has not written the most original poetry, nor the most lyrical, nor the profoundest, nor the most humorous, nor the most vibrant—the list could be extended—for one must take into account Ted Hughes, the venerable Robert Graves, Philip Larkin, Sir John Betjeman, and Stevie Smith among others. If it is possible to generalize about poets as diverse as those named, then it can be said these artists succeed on the whole by working a narrow and particularized approach. This is by way of identifying Fuller as a normalized generalist. Fuller's high profile

134

representativeness is both his strength (and value) and limitation as a poet. Fuller does not lift the reader out of his being and does not afford him unusual or striking ways of apprehending experience; he does enable the reader to comprehend more penetratingly and feelingly a reality approximating his own sense of it. If he does not take the reader out of himself he permits him to more fully possess himself. Fuller has a worldliness, a flexibility, a balance, a totality of being not found in Hughes or Graves or Smith. This may make, finally, for a less impressive kind of poetry in a literary sense, but produces nonetheless moving and meaningful work in a humane one. Is it a fair kind of analogy to suggest that one would be more excited to meet Hughes or Graves than Fuller, but one would choose Fuller for extended personal friendship?

Fuller has looked out at his times with astuteness and honesty, with generosity and perspective, and anyone who considers the longevity of his career is bound to be struck by his resilience. The thirties, the war years, the aftermath, the truculent sixties— for forty years he has sustained unflagging fascination with life, essentially the "little" life surrounding him as a suburban Londoner, essentially the out-of-sight life of responses to his life in time. Some may believe the times are best reflected in the tramps of Beckett and Pinter. I see the omniverously intellectual Fuller voicing the worries and concerns, the good sense and joy-in-life-despite-everything outlook of masses of thoughtful people. And he has sustained it without the least sense of trivialization or sentimentalism.

Most succinctly, Robert Garfitt expresses admiration for Fuller's resilience in defining and redefining his values with humane openness: "His has always been an embattled vision: equally, it has never ceased to reckon with its own contradictions, and to admit of change. What is remarkable in his work is not so much the stamina with which his themes have been sustained as that rarer kind of energy which has allowed them continually to be broken down and renewed within a complex and evolving dialogue."[1]

Of the contemporaries I have named, Larkin is of course closest to Fuller in his affinity for the commonplace. Larkin handles this largely from the inside and with great specificity and consequently his verse has an emotive force that exceeds that found or intended in Fuller's work. Fuller is detached and exploratory and accordingly cooler and inevitably ironic. As has been noted, "In common with most of the intellectual Left, Roy Fuller suffered an imaginative estrangement from those to whom he was intellectually committed."[2] To restate an observation made early in this study, Fuller is the preeminent British ruminative poet of his age.

I have insisted throughout on the homogeniety of Fuller's work, on the smooth continuity of the entire career; yet it is appropriate at the close to challenge this by noting there are several different Fullers, as, indeed, we might reasonably expect of a writer whose career spans four decades. Fuller has been frequently generalized as a politically oriented writer and while this description is founded on solid evidence it is too facile and delimiting. Fuller has not been different at various junctures of his career so much as capable of interchanging his concerns and attitudes at any point. He has written notable occasional or public verse; but the present survey demonstrates a very high percentage of light verse. He has been a nature poet, a spokesman for what I have termed the anagogical states, he has been an endearing voyeur, and he has been preeminent as a poet who has made poetry out of illness and not the fact so much as the process of aging. Throughout his career he has been a craftsman of a high order who has neither eschewed established poetic forms nor hesitated to experiment with such challenges as those posed by syllabic versification.

This study might be said to have had its beginning in Stephen Spender's description of Fuller as "a norm against whom other poets of the past thirty years may be judged." Now we come full circle, trusting that this central insight has been amply validated.

I have already indicated that in my view, *My Child, My Sister* is Fuller's principal novel, followed by *The Ruined Boys*; it is appropriate to conclude with my short list of his finest poetry. This list is arranged chronologically by volumes and intended to provide a representative sampling across his whole career: "To My Brother," "To My Wife," "Sadness, Theory, Glass," "The Statue," "The Image," "Translation," "The Perturbations of Uranus," "The Final Period," "The Ides of March," "Mythological Sonnets," "Meredithian Sonnets," "Monologue in Autumn," "Versions of Love," "To X," "At T. S. Eliot's Memorial Service," "Tiny Tears."

Notes and References

Chapter One

1. Roy Fuller, "Poetry in My Time," *Essays by Divers Hands* (Oxford, 1968), p. 68.
2. Peter Firchow, ed., *The Writer's Place* (Minneapolis, 1974), pp. 134–35.
3. Ibid., p. 128.
4. "Poetry in My Time," p. 68.
5. Ibid.
6. Firchow, pp. 123–24.
7. Ian Hamilton, "Professor of Poetry," *The Listener*, 5 Dec. 1968, p. 762.
8. Roy Fuller, "From Blackheath to Oxford," *London Magazine*, March 1969, p. 25.
9. Hamilton, p. 762.
10. Edward Lucie-Smith, ed., *British Poetry since 1945* (Harmondsworth, 1970), p. 110.
11. *New Statesman*, 28 Sept. 1962, p. 410.
12. "From Blackheath to Oxford," p. 24.
13. Ibid.
14. Ibid.
15. "Poetry in My Time," p. 68.
16. Ibid.
17. Ibid., p. 70.
18. Peter Orr, ed., "Roy Fuller," *The Poet Speaks* (London, 1966), p. 65.
19. "Poetry in My Time," p. 71.
20. George Woodcock, "Private Images of Public Ills: The Poetry of Roy Fuller," *Wascana Review*, 4, No. 2 (1969), 22.
21. Ibid.
22. Firchow, p. 127.
23. Orr, p. 64.
24. Julian Symons, "Weighing Room," *London Magazine*, April–May 1976, p. 106.
25. Lucie-Smith, p. 110.
26. Hamilton, p. 761.
30. "From Blackheath to Oxford," p. 25.

31. "Poetry in My Time," p. 76.

32. John Press, *Rule and Energy, Trends in British Poetry since the Second World War* (London, 1963), p. 161.

33. "Poetry in My Time," p. 78.

34. G. S. Fraser, "English Poetry 1930-1960," *The Twentieth Century,* ed. Bernard Bergonzi (London, 1970), p. 303.

35. "In the Movement," *Spectator,* Oct. 1954, p. 400.

36. Fraser, p. 303.

37. David Timms, *Philip Larkin* (Edinburgh, 1973), p. 12.

38. Lucie-Smith, p. 110.

39. "Poetry in My Time," p. 79.

40. Stephen Spender, "From Marx to Faust," *London Magazine,* Feb. 1963, p. 72.

41. Ibid.

42. *Times Literary Supplement,* 31 Aug. 1962, p. 656.

43. Ibid., 3 Jan. 1958, p. 9.

44. Spender, p. 72.

45. Ibid.

46. Woodcock, p. 24.

47. Valentine Cunningham, "Prudence Farmer Poetry Prize," *New Statesman,* 30 July 1976, p. 153.

48. Orr, p. 67.

49. *Times Literary Supplement,* 3 Jan. 1958, p. 9.

50. "Poetry in My Time," p. 77.

Chapter Two

1. Roger Garfitt, "Intimate Anxieties," *London Magazine,* 15 (Dec. 1975-Jan. 1976), 102.

2. *Times Literary Supplement,* 31 Aug. 1962, p. 656.

3. Press, p. 165.

4. Garfitt, p. 104.

5. Press, p. 168.

Chapter Three

1. Mentioned by Fuller in conversation with me July 1973.

2. Garfitt, p. 107.

3. Ibid., p. 108.

Chapter Four

1. Garfitt, p. 108.

2. Ibid.

3. George Macbeth, ed., *Poetry 1900 to 1965* (London, 1967), p. 212.

4. Ian Hamilton, *A Poetry Chronicle* (London, 1973).

5. Hamilton, p. 89.

6. John Fuller is the author of *The Reader's Guide to W. H. Auden.*

7. Shortly after the publication of *Tiny Tears,* which included these seven poems "from an old file," Fuller published in 1974 a pamphet, *An Old War,* at the Tragara Press, Edinburgh, containing seven more poems from the same file. In a prefatory note the poet indicates they were written during the war but never previously published.

8. *Poetry Book Society Bulletin,* No. 85 (Summer, 1975), p. 2.

9. *Poetry Book Society Bulletin,* p. 2.

10. Following the publication of *From the Joke Shop,* a pamphet, *The Joke Shop Annexe,* limited to 115 copies, was published by the Tragara Press, Edinburgh. It contains five poems which, but for their lateness, would have been included in the volume proper, "though possibly not," the author remarks in an introductory note, "at the very end as indicated by the numbering here."

Chapter Five

1. *Times Literary Supplement,* 20 Mar. 1959, p. 166.

2. Firchow, p. 135.

3. Fuller told me in conversation that the film rights to *The Carnal Island* have been purchased by Joseph Losey and that he understood there had been talk of casting James Mason in the role of Daniel House.

Chapter Seven

1. Garfitt, p. 102.

2. Ibid., p. 105.

Selected Bibliography

PRIMARY SOURCES

1. Poetry
Poems. London: Fortune Press, 1939.
The Middle of a War. London: Hogarth Press, 1942.
A Lost Season. London: Hogarth Press, 1944.
Epitaphs and Occasions. London: John Lehmann, 1949.
Counterparts. London: Derek Verschoyle, 1954.
Brutus's Orchard. London: André Deutsch, 1957.
Collected Poems. London: André Deutsch, 1962.
Buff. London: André Deutsch, 1965.
New Poems. London: André Deutsch, 1968.
Tiny Tears. London: André Deutsch, 1973.
An Old War. Edinburgh: Tragara Press, 1974.
From the Joke Shop. London: André Deutsch, 1975.
The Joke Shop Annexe. Edinburgh: Tragara Press, 1975.

2. Fiction
Savage Gold. London: Hutchinson, 1946.
With My Little Eye. London: John Lehmann, 1948.
The Second Curtain. London: Derek Verschoyle, 1953.
Fantasy and Fugue. London: Derek Verschoyle, 1954.
Image of a Society. London. André Deutsch, 1956.
The Ruined Boys. London: André Deutsch, 1959.
The Father's Comedy. London: André Deutsch, 1961.
The Perfect Fool. London: André Deutsch, 1963.
My Child, My Sister. London: André Deutsch, 1965.
Catspaw. London: Alan Ross, 1966.
The Carnal Island. London: André Deutsch, 1970.

3. Nonfiction
Owls and Artificers. London: André Deutsch, 1971.
Professors and Gods. London: André Deutsch, 1973.

SECONDARY SOURCES

This selective list excludes reviews.

FIRCHOW, PETER, ed. *The Writer's Place*. Minneapolis: University of Minnesota Press, 1974. An informative interview emphasizing the problems of being a writer in contemporary England.

FRASER, G. S. "English Poetry 1930-1960." *In The Twentieth Century*. Ed. Bernard Bergonzi. London: Sphere, 1970. Brief but judicious contextual treatment.

GARFITT, ROGER. "Intimate Anxieties." *London Magazine,* 15 (Dec. 1975-1976), 102-09. Brief but comprehensive, this is the best discussion of the poetry to date.

HAMILTON, IAN. "Professor of Poetry." *The Listener, 5, Dec. 1968, pp. 761-62. Chiefly biographical with several revealing quotations from Fuller.*

ORR, PETER, ed., *The Poet Speaks. Interviews with Contemporary Poets.* London: Routledge & Kegan Paul 1966. Fuller proves very forthright in talking about both himself and his work.

PRESS, JOHN. *A Map of Modern English Verse.* London: Oxford University Press, 1969. Places the poet in the literary context of his time.

———. *Rule and Energy. Trends in British Poetry since the Second World War.* London: Oxford University Press, 1963. Emphasizes the metaphysical qualities which the author discerns in the poetry.

THWAITE, ANTHONY. *Contemporary English Poetry.* London: Heinemann, 1964. Brief but astute discussion of the poetry.

WOODCOCK, GEORGE. "Private Images of Public Ills: The Poetry of Roy Fuller." *Wascana Review,* 4, No. 2 (1969), 21-34. Especially informative on the poetic situation of the thirties, this is a penetrating discussion of the earlier poetry.

Index

142